First hand experience
what matters to children

An alphabet of learning from the real world

With a foreword by Tim Smit, Chief Executive, The Eden Project

by **Diane Rich**
Denise Casanova
Annabelle Dixon
Mary Jane Drummond
Andrea Durrant
Cathy Myer

We dedicate this book to our dear friend and colleague

Annabelle Dixon
(1940–2005)

in memory of her work with children and adult educators

Published in 2005 by
Rich Learning Opportunities
IP13 6SH, UK

www.richlearningopportunities.co.uk

ISBN 0-9549683-0-1

© Rich Learning Opportunities and
The What Matters to Children Team 2005

Produced by Expression, IP23 8HH, UK
Additional copies are available from www.richlearningopportunities.co.uk

Email office@richlearningopportunities.co.uk

Contents

Acknowledgements

Materials in this book have been trialled by 66 educators from 18 different settings, in eight LEAs.

The authors are very grateful to all those who gave up their time to come to meetings, and to work in their settings with children, parents, colleagues and governors, to introduce and work with these materials and provide valuable feedback.

The settings represent a mixture of rural, urban and multicultural areas. A variety of educators took part, including headteachers, centre managers, class teachers, support staff, nursery nurses and class room assistants. They include staff from:
Abbotsmede Primary School *Peterborough*
Capel St Mary Primary School *Suffolk*
Coton Primary School *Cambridgeshire*
Crabtree Infant School *Hertfordshire*
George Street Primary School *Hertfordshire*
Highfield Nursery School *Suffolk*
Histon Infant School *Cambridgeshire*
Icknield Infant and Nursery School *Hertfordshire*
Kingshill Infant School *Hertfordshire*
Malorees Infant School *Brent*
Low Hall Nursery School *Waltham Forest*
South Axholme Peripatetic Nursery *Doncaster*
Thongsley Fields Primary and Nursery School *Cambridgeshire*
Tottenhall Infant and Nursery School *Enfield*
The Grove Primary School *Enfield*
The Wroxham School *Hertfordshire*
Westfield First School *Hertfordshire*
Wickham Market Primary and Nursery School *Suffolk*

Those taking part were:
Cheryl Barlow, Ann Blanchard, Frances Chesnick, Ana Clark, Clare Clarke, Sarah Clark, Sian Davies, Sarah Day, Vicky Dean, Charlotte Devereux, Judy Dunne, Margaret Dunlop, Liz Du Toit, Lynne Edwards, Jacqueline Egan, Sue Fenwick, Christine Fulcher, Gemma Fry, Helena Garibaldinos, Jenny Gordon, Belinda Handley, Laura Harrisskitt, Anne Hawkins, Hilary Hollick, Lynne Howell, Bernie Jackson, Helen Laws, Marion Leeper, Jenny Maguire, Judy Major, Eileen Martin, Melanie Mathison, Julie Mellor, Ann Mitchell, Cristina Modestou, Rachel Myer, Lucy Newton, Carol Nind, Suzanne Odhams, Sue Papaspyru, Maria Park, Alison Peacock, Terry Pearson, Wendy Perry, Caroline Price, Sarah Roberson, Ann Robinett, Alison Rowbotham, Tessa Roworth, Sue Shaw, Tricia Shingles, Karen Spring, Sonal Thakore, Carly Tilney, Sharron Tingey, Claire Toberman, Rachael Tomlin, Ann Warren, Jane Whitehurst, Susan Williams, Helena Worley, Georgina Wray, Rosemary Zelli.
There may be other educators who supported those listed above, whose names we have not been given. We are grateful to them for their support.

Thanks to Mary Naylor and Andrea Sully for additional materials.

Grateful thanks to Jane Lane for her useful comments on drafts and to Jenny Howard for initial proof reading.

The authors and publisher are grateful to
• Bloodaxe Books, Northumberland for permission to include the poem *Oh Taste and See* by Denise Levertov.
• Great Ormond Street Hospital Children's Charity (1937) for permission to include an excerpt from *Peter Pan and Wendy* by J. M. Barrie.
• Random House for permission to include an excerpt from *Island* by Aldous Huxley.

About the authors

The authors are a team of experienced and respected education consultants. They have come together to work on a variety of projects for many years, and have always been committed to promoting what matters to children.

Diane Rich has been involved in children's learning for many years, as play worker, teacher, advisory teacher, researcher, consultant, author, trustee for children's charities, former Chief Executive of a national early years charity. She runs *Rich Learning Opportunities: keeping creativity, play and first hand experience at the heart of children's learning*.

Denise Casanova is an artist and freelance arts education consultant who is committed to education through the arts. She has taught extensively for schools, museums and arts organisations in the USA and UK.

Annabelle Dixon's classroom was, in the words of a friend, 'a place of genuine intellectual search.' As psychologist and teacher she was committed to offering first hand experiences to children as the essential basis for such a search.

Mary Jane Drummond is a writer and researcher with an abiding interest in young children's learning. She has recently retired from the Faculty of Education at the University of Cambridge.

Andrea Durrant has taught both children and teachers. She is now a freelance consultant in early years and primary education. Her mission is to bring back creativity into children's learning.

Cathy Myer has been a teacher, advisory teacher and university lecturer. She is now a freelance education consultant, passionate about children and their capacity to learn from their experiences of the real world.

A note about terms

Throughout this book we use the term **educators** to refer all those who work with children aged three to eight: carers, childminders, play workers, nursery nurses, teachers, classroom assistants, students.

We use the term **setting** to refer to any permanent location where educators work with children.

All those who are significant carers for children at home are referred to as **parents**.

Our definition of **inclusion** is taken from the statement agreed in June 2003 by the Early Childhood Forum which states that:

> …inclusion is a process of identifying, understanding and breaking down the barriers to participation and belonging.
> (Dickens, M. and Denziloe J. 2003)

Foreword
Pain, love, loss, looking and learning

by Tim Smit

There is a famous doggerel Confucian saying which holds that 'wise men do not learn from experience, but from the experience of others'. It sounds good, but like so much marketing speak it is only a partial truth. For instance, you don't need to bang your head on a brick wall to know that it hurts, but the same is not true of the generic need to experience pain; only by going through it do you know how much you can take and what you might be able to put up with in survival situations. The same is true of almost any fear; confronting it is often the only way to deal with it and to grow as an individual. Many people suffer agonies of insecurity in later life because they have avoided anything unpleasant. The fear of fear creates in them a paralysis that inhibits their dealings with people and situations; this ultimately leads to a greater unhappiness than if they had dealt with pain head on, for themselves.

I start from a serious premise in order to put experience into context. In any situation, both passive observer and active participant are subject to an experience. The former learns vicariously from the lived experience of the other. The latter experiences it directly, but in being so focused may not see the whole. Each will have learned different things. I am arguing that both kinds of learning from experience are important in building up a palette of responses to a huge range of situations, but the lessons are qualitatively different when they concern cause and effect – the consequences for one's feelings, both physical and emotional. These are exclusive to the participant. To say that it is better to have loved and lost than never to have loved at all can only be said and meant by someone who has loved, for the observed behaviour of the abandoned lover would appear to contradict it!

My childhood was rich in smells, noises, warmth and little frissons of terror – mostly of my own making. I climbed trees with daring, but was hugely frightened. I lifted stones wherever I went in order to inhale the smell of moist earth and the slightly lemony hay smell of crushed bracken. My thrills were slow worms and toads. There was pond dipping and racing water boatmen, catching sticklebacks and grazing my knees falling off bicycles and out of trees. I spent hours banging random chords on pianos and imagining the worlds to which they formed the soundtrack. Often I took my shoes off and loved the tickly feeling of cut grass, the swishy feeling of long grass, the irresistible roughness of hard sand, and the exotic caress of dry sand; but most of all there was mud. How glorious to let it squidge through your toes! And peeling it off when it dried was another sensation altogether.

David Byrne, of the American group Talking Heads, once wrote a profound song called, I think, 'The Naming of Things'. It describes a young child in a garden listening happily to the birdsong. When his mother sits down and names each bird, the child can hear it no more, until eventually the garden is silent to him. This is a profoundly melancholy notion; I suppose it matches the cautionary tale about the man who knows the price of everything, but the value of nothing. It's funny though, that as I have got older, I realise that I have to work harder at enjoying simple pleasures, because I have become self-conscious of them.

The most important single event in my sensory life was when a good friend asked me to give him one hour of my time to do exactly as he demanded. I trusted him and agreed. He took me to a field and marked out a metre square of grass. He made me sit and asked me to stare at it for a full hour, maintaining my concentration. To start with I saw grass. Then I saw a spider, then an ant, more ants, more spiders, beetles, a shrew, and within the hour my world had turned upside down. I had looked through the keyhole at a micro-world heaving with life, all of it oblivious of me. How was it possible that I had been so unaware of this complexity? Don't get me wrong, I knew a fair bit about ecology, but knowing it as a theory, and really being aware of it and feeling it, are different.

From that moment on I have been an angry man. My target is all those sloppy people who casually use phrases such as 'the world is so much busier and faster today'. I rant at them and I sneer. How many paces is it from your front door to the gate? How many lamp posts are there on your street? What colour is the light? I take my young Eden Project team members down to the pub on a Friday. 'What are you trying to achieve with the project?' they ask, bright eyed and keen. 'Close your eyes,' I demand. They do as they're asked. 'Please describe the person next to you; colour of eyes, jewellery, hair and so on. Tell me what is on the table. The beer you are drinking: where do the bubbles form – on the side or in the middle? What colour is it? If you must smoke, tell me, how does the smoke curl?' Stunned, most of them fail the test miserably. Strangely, it always appears that the quietest among them seem to have most of the answers now. The mouthy ones are lost. This is a great lesson for any leader; don't confuse quiet or shy with the absence of something to say.

This, I declare, is one of the major things the Eden Project is about. Observation. It is both the foundation of all good science and also the basis for learning from your experience. The world is no faster today than it has ever been. We are merely skating quickly over the top rather than dealing with it or understanding what it is.

'Older and wiser'. There's a phrase. With age you just get older unless you observe closely and allow yourself to feel. Travel broadens the mind – or, does it? To tick off the Pyramids and the Taj Mahal is nothing if you can't feel anything, sense anything, save the thrill of having seen it. No more significant than answering a question correctly on a quiz show. However there are two common phrases I can recommend, 'waste not, want not'– for here, you are living with the grain of nature. And 'variety is the spice of life' – for here lies enlightenment and the only way of knowing this to be true is to experience it both passively and actively, for yourself.

First hand experience is perhaps the most important foundation stone in discovering who you really are, and what you might become. Without huge dollops of it, encouraged and nurtured, but rarely directed, we can never become more than the sum of other people's lives, experienced at second hand. The nightmare vision of a world of non-biologically related clones is an hysterical oversimplification of a possible future. The antidote is to take a few risks, and to let the mud squidge through your toes from time to time. Read this book. It may save lives.

Tim Smit
Chief Executive, The Eden Project
Bodelva
Cornwall
PL24 2SG
www.edenproject.com

The Eden Project. Home of the Eden Trust. Charity No. 1093070

Part One
Introduction

What is this book?

This book is an alphabet of first hand experiences. The text for each letter has been designed as a springboard from which children and educators can launch themselves into the beautiful, mysterious, physical world in which we all live, looking and listening, tasting, touching, and breathing it in.

Why did we write it?

There is no shortage of advice and guidance for educators working with children from three to eight years of age. Our intention in adding to these materials is to support educators in thinking more deeply about one particular aspect of children's learning in those years: their active learning, which is stimulated by high quality first hand experiences.

In recent times, many early years educators in England have been affected by downward pressures from Key Stage 1 (KS1) and beyond; in KS1 the pressure to achieve high SATS results for six and seven year olds is undeniably affecting the breadth and balance of activities offered to children, with achievements in the core subjects prioritised over active experiences in the foundation subjects. The national literacy and numeracy strategies in England have also had an effect on the overall experience of children in their first years of schooling.

It is within this context that we have observed, over the last few years, a decrease in the opportunities offered to children to experience *at first hand* aspects of the real world, from outside the four walls of their educational setting. Inside the setting we see copious paper and pencil activities, and sitting down at a table activities; we see children looking at images on computer screens, and cutting pictures out of magazines and catalogues, without experiencing the reality for which these images stand. In classrooms for four and five year olds, we have seen a lesson on taste where there was nothing to taste and a lesson on materials where there were no materials. We have seen a lesson on babies and toddlers without any living babies, and a lesson on pets using images of pets downloaded from the Internet. The lesson plans did not include living experiences to support these second-hand activities.

In a recent study of children's experiences in reception classes (*Inside the Foundation Stage* Adams et al 2004) one of us has documented the rarity of authentic first hand experiences in a small sample of classrooms in England. Using both quantitative and qualitative methods to analyse 25 hours of target-child observations, the researchers conclude that there is an urgent need to reinstate first hand experience as a core element of every child's entitlement in early education settings.

These findings and our own continuing observations have caused us much concern. As we discussed our perceptions of the issues with the experienced educators with whom we work, we listened sympathetically to their accounts of the constraints that prevent them, as they see it, from providing authentic first hand experiences, on a regular basis, across the curriculum, for all children. Educators talked about the pressures to cover all the learning objectives, to provide evidence, in the form of written work, for every objective, to meet targets, to raise literacy and numeracy standards, to work within the guidelines of the national strategies, to prepare for, and survive, Ofsted inspections, and to complete detailed short, medium and long-term planning sheets. Their thoughtful, sometimes rueful, comments encouraged us to continue with the writing of this book, convinced that we could offer something of value to educators looking for support and sustenance in order to work in ways that more actively engage children in exploring the world – and everything and everyone in it. As we see it, this book stands alongside both the current curriculum guidance for the Foundation Stage, and the National Curriculum documents for KS1, extending and expanding their references to, for example, 'real life situations' (QCA 2000 p15). But its use is not restricted to English settings, since it can also support educators all over the world.

The structure of the book

The pages of the second part of this book are of three different kinds:
- Alphabet pages
- Learning stories
- I K L Q T Z: these pages are different

Alphabet pages

These pages use the same format; they are divided into a number of boxes, each containing concise suggestions for exploring the headline topic (for example, **A is for apples**, **B is for brushes** and so on). The elements that make up each page are the outcomes of our analysis of the problem as we see it, and our considered views on how best to tackle it. These elements include:
- what matters to children
- verbs and nouns (things to do and investigate)
- big ideas
- questions worth asking
- books and stories

Each of these is described briefly below. The most important of them is our understanding of what matters to children.

What matters to children

Our analysis of what matters to children is at the heart of everything we have written. We are convinced that simply providing 'things for children to do' is an inadequate description of what needs to be done to improve children's opportunities to experience the world at first hand. Our position is that the things children do, while they are three to eight years old, should be the things that really matter to them, not the things that matter to their educators, or to the authors of helpful advice on provision and resources. Our own thinking about what

matters to children is described in full on the page for the letter 'I' which we have used to stand for the active learner, the child at the centre of the whole process of education. It includes:

- what is in the world
- who is in the world
- touching and tasting the world
- knowing the world
- making sense of the world
- exploring how things work
- moving about in the world
- acting on the world and making a mark on it
- being engaged, with authentic purposes
- being with friends
- being in different kinds of places
- making collections
- having a sense of big belonging
- making my own world map and my own moral map
- finding out what the world is made of
- being in the world of living things
- understanding how the world works
- finding out how to keep safe in the world.

'What matters to children' is also represented on every page of this alphabet: we have used these ideas as strict criteria for the suggestions we make for each area of enquiry.

Food and exercise: verbs and nouns

Our thinking about the early years curriculum and the content of the alphabet pages that follow has been influenced by a vivid metaphor used by more than one eminent writer on child development: food and exercise. In this book we conceptualise the curriculum for young children first, in terms of a nourishing diet of first hand experiences, and secondly, in terms of manifold opportunities for children to exercise their growing powers to do, to think, to understand and to act on the world in ways of their own invention. Accordingly on each page of this book there are lists of verbs, suggesting the kinds of active exercise that children could and should take in each area of enquiry. These lists are headed, variously; FIND, COLLECT, INVESTIGATE, VISIT, MAKE and so on. There are also other lists of nouns, nouns that suggest the actual things, people, plants and animals that children could and should encounter in their enquiries.

Big ideas: towards conceptual growth

Our metaphor of food and exercise takes us a little further than nouns and verbs. Accordingly, we also include on each page an outline of the conceptual food that we consider each topic to be best suited to provide. These lists of big ideas show how, in studying small and everyday elements of the real world, children are also learning to think about big ideas, important ideas with a part to play in their full-time project of making sense of the world, how it works and how it can be made a better place for everyone. We see children, as the work of Gordon Wells has so convincingly demonstrated, as capable and hard-working meaning-makers, continuously building up their understanding of the concepts that hold the world together (Wells 1987).

Questions worth asking

On each page we offer some suggestions for puzzling and challenging issues that might arise in the course of children's enquiries. We are NOT suggesting that these questions should be presented to children as they stand, OR that children should be required to answer them, every last one. We ARE suggesting that every topic in this book has the potential to throw up paradoxical and enticing topics for discussion, in the form of questions that should not be answered by an internet search, but only by extended discussion, debate and exploration. Children's own questions are often of this kind, and are an especially fruitful starting point for the kind of thinking-out-loud we are advocating here. This topic is taken further on the pages headed Q is for questions.

Books and stories

In these boxes we offer suggestions for appropriate books and stories that could be used to deepen and broaden children's enquiries and interests. For all that this book's principal concern is with the real world, and children's first hand experience of that world, we firmly believe that children's learning can always be enriched by the world of books: by poetry, myth, fairy-tale, fable, legend, adventure, romance, dreams and domestic drama. Writers are able to express experiences that we are unable to put into words. Reading their words, or hearing them read aloud, can deepen and confirm our understanding of the experience itself. Every story tells a truth about major experiences and feelings, such as fear and courage, anticipation, joy, being different, disappointment and rejection, being found wanting and being labelled, love, hate, good and evil. Stories and poems that reflect these emotions will assure listeners and readers that they are not alone and that their experience is valid and real and that empathy, comfort and security are powerfully present in the world.

The role of the educator

The brief discussion of curriculum content given above leads us to our view of the role of the educator; we see it in terms of three pressing responsibilities – *to provide, to organise and to value* (Drummond 1996). First, it is the educator's responsibility to provide the curricular food that will nourish and strengthen children's powers; their second responsibility is to organise children's enquiries and experiences so that they are actively and emotionally engaged, exploring those aspects of the world that really matter to them, for themselves, with their own hands and eyes and ears and voices, with their own observations, theories, experiments, discoveries and critical questions. And thirdly, through the regular practice of systematic observation, educators learn to value the learning that they see going on before their eyes. They are then in a powerful position to document that worthwhile learning, for the eyes of their colleagues, for parents, and for all interested others. Educators will then be able to articulate the value of that learning, making a serious and convincing case for the quality of what they provide and organise. They will be able to use their observations to plan their next steps, taking account of children's growing understanding and expanding horizons, and matching their plans to children's interests and concerns.

The world that children encounter, inside and outside their settings, is far from perfect: inequity and injustice are deeply embedded within society. It is the additional responsibility of all educators to be aware that the concepts of equality and inclusion are of paramount importance in their settings and local communities. Of course, this does not imply that every educator is personally responsible for the influences of the wider world on children and their families. But rather, educators have a responsibility to recognise and acknowledge these inequalities and to commit themselves to working to remove all barriers to social justice.

We see this further responsibility in terms of educators recognising and responding to opportunities for children to learn about prejudice, discrimination, and unfairness. Sometimes this means they will unlearn unexamined, negative attitudes to difference and diversity. First hand experience of prejudice, discrimination and injustice are painful and damaging; but they are not to be denied or ignored. They can be seen as opportunities for educators to challenge the pervading hierarchies of language, skin colour, gender, culture, religion, ethnicity, disability, in which some people are more highly valued than others. Educators who express their critical awareness of these issues and who are willing to challenge inequity, play an important part in children learning to live by the values of the harmonious and inclusive society that they deserve.

Learning stories

The book does not include detailed suggestions for classroom organisation, for planning, or for ways of managing this approach. There are already many useful texts on these themes; we have chosen instead to emphasise particular kinds of learning, the learning that is stimulated and fostered by the sustained and continuous provision of authentic first hand experiences. However, in the section that follows, about how to use this book, there is a brief explanation of how we envisage this approach in action. In addition, most of the alphabet pages are accompanied by detailed 'learning stories'. Some are examples of the work of a group of educators who were invited to trial the materials and contribute to the text. Others are contributions offered by educators who are committed to promoting first hand experience with children. On these pages, readers will find educators accounts of children learning from first hand experiences: we have called these pages 'learning stories' in recognition of the ground-

breaking work of Margaret Carr and her colleagues in New Zealand in assessing and documenting children's learning (Carr 2001). These accounts also illustrate the planning and organisation strategies used by our contributors, who have participated in putting this approach into practice and who have fascinating learning and teaching stories to tell.

Focus on learning

The alphabet pages of this book are about experiences and opportunities that might stimulate many different kinds of worthwhile learning; the activities we suggest are essentially open-ended and it is impossible to define in advance the learning that will take place as children engage with their enquiries. But we have included one page with a brief analysis of the learning that might result from a study of bags and brushes, along with some comments on the educator's part in supporting and encouraging that learning (see p.27, immediately after the pages for the letter B).

Snappy quotes

Because this is not a conventional book for educators, built up of successive chapters of continuous prose, we have not included a conventional reading list, although we do provide references for all the authorities we mention in the text. Less conventionally, we have also included on every page short, memorable quotations from an eclectic range of thinkers whose work is important to us. We hope our use of quotations will motivate educators to follow up the ideas of those who inspire them – or challenge or provoke. We are not suggesting that every educator should agree with every quotation we use: disagreement and debate are sometimes the most fruitful responses to a new idea - just as learning to understand someone else's viewpoint can be an important part of reflective practice.

I K L Q T Z – these pages are different

I is for the active learner

On this page we emphasise our view of children as active learners, who do their own thinking, planning, choosing, making, doing and understanding. Here we outline our analysis of 'what matters to children' and what kinds of learning are most worthwhile.

K is for knowing

On this page we acknowledge the importance of the kinds of knowing emphasised by some current guidance documents, particularly for early literacy and numeracy, and argue that, in addition, there are other important kinds of knowledge, linked to the kinds of knowing that matter to children: in particular, knowing, how, who, when, where and why. These kinds of knowing entail, in their turn, learning about many of the conflicts and inequalities that characterise our world; children's thirst for learning encompasses knowing who not, as well as who, how not, as well as how, where not as well as where and importantly, why not, as well as why.

L is for looking and listening

On this page we argue that every first hand activity engaged in by children involves listening and looking of some kind, sometimes many kinds. We outline the characteristics of worthwhile listening and looking, maintaining that children also need plenty of opportunity and encouragement to talk about what they see and hear, and to express their thinking in different ways. This applies to blind and deaf children too, who like all children, will be listening and looking with all their senses.

Q is for questions

On these pages we discuss the characteristics of questions that genuinely stimulate children's thinking and understanding, and explain our use of a box on every page labelled 'Questions worth asking'. We also consider the importance of children's questions and describe the educator's role in encouraging children to voice their powerful questions, some of them difficult ones, about the world. We detail a practical approach to children's questions used by one of the project team, explaining how children's questions can be used as the starting points for structured enquiry.

T is for thinking

On this page we summarise some of our own thoughts about children's thinking, the important kinds of thinking that are stimulated and fostered by the first hand experiences we are promoting on the other alphabet pages.

Z is for zig-zag

On this final page we re-emphasise the underlying propositions about children as learners on which the whole book is based, and describe the way in which educators might plan a zig-zag route through the alphabet pages. Although the alphabet comes to an end on this page, we hope that educators who read this far will not see their work as suddenly coming to a close. We warmly encourage educators to build on their experiences of using this book, and to continue to act as critically aware, observant, reflective and inventive supporters of children's learning, offering them countless first hand experiences to feed their insatiable appetite for the world.

Encouraging voices, old and new: the theoretical underpinnings of our work

This book has its roots in documents that were once seen as seminal. In particular we have returned to the Plowden Report, *Children and their Primary Schools*, published in 1967, which was read by many teachers, for many years, as a distillation of all that was excellent in contemporary primary education. Whether this condition of excellence ever existed in more than a small minority of schools is debatable, but some of the aspects of the 'Plowden School' are, we believe, just as desirable today, as they were nearly 40 years ago.

For example:

> A school is not merely a teaching shop; it must transmit values and attitudes…The school sets out deliberately to devise the right environment for children, to allow them to be themselves and to develop in the way and the pace appropriate to them…It lays special stress on individual discovery, on first hand experience, and opportunities for creative work. It insists that knowledge does not fall into neatly separate compartments and that work and play are not opposite but complementary.
>
> (CACE 1967: 187-8)

It is worth noting that this emphasis on discovery and first hand experiences in an appropriate environment had already appeared in an earlier, equally significant report, the *Hadow Report on Infant and Nursery*

Schools, published in 1933. Some memorable passages from this report are especially relevant to the task we have set ourselves in this book:

> The curriculum is to be thought of in terms of activity and experience, rather than of knowledge and facts to be stored… What we desire to see is the acceptance of a different set of values from that which has been usual in the past; less weight on the imparting of an ordered body of knowledge and more on the development of the child's innate powers, less reliance on the artificial life of the classroom, more on the experience to be gained out of doors and the opportunities for experiment and discovery which close contact with the real world provides.
>
> (Board of Education 1933: 117-23)

More recent official publications have echoed the theme of first hand experience, but in rather less emphatic terms. The QCA (2000) *Curriculum Guidance for the Foundation Stage*, now in use in Foundation Stage settings in England, recommends that children should be offered experiences 'mostly based on real life situations' (p.15), and elsewhere calls for 'rich and stimulating experiences' (p.14). Curriculum frameworks in other countries make similar references to first hand experience. In Scotland, for example, the general principles that underpin the *Scottish Office Curriculum Framework 3–5* (1999) lead to the recommendation that 'pre-school education should aim to…encourage children to explore, appreciate and respect their environment' (p.2) and the *The Structure and Balance of the Curriculum: 5–14 National Guidelines (Scotland)* (2000) recommends that provision should 'relate to events and facets of [children's] everyday lives' (p.9). These phrases remind us of what the sadly neglected *Rumbold Report* (DES 1990) so powerfully recommended: 'an approach to learning which emphasises first hand experiences and which views play and talk as powerful mediums for learning'. The 2003 DfES document *Excellence and Enjoyment: a strategy for primary schools* emphasises the importance of 'a rich and exciting curriculum for children' throughout. The six principles of learning and teaching set out in the same document state that, 'Good learning and teaching should…make learning vivid and real'.

Even these brief and selective quotations from official sources are enough to demonstrate that this book is, in an important sense, a reminder of some things we used to know about children's learning, and their need for real world experiences, rather than a radical new departure.

We were equally encouraged in our work by many other authors, some of whose words we have used at intervals throughout the book. Robin Hodgkin's work, in *Playing and Exploring*, (Hodgkin 1985) was also a source of affirmation for what we are trying to do.

> Rather than ask 'what stick or carrot will make children active in certain ways?' or 'what will make them go in this direction rather than that?' we would do well to turn the problem round and to say: children will go in any case, for it is an expression of their being to be purposeful and energetic.
>
> (Hodgkin 1985)

Inspiration of a different kind came from the English-born poet and philosopher Denise Levertov, reminding us of our original concern, and powerfully describing her visionary solution to the problem.

We discussed this poem, 'O Taste and See', at an early meeting of the project team. One of us had recently visited an infant school set in the grounds of an extensive orchard. It was a bright blue September day, and the trees were groaning with fruit; the grass was full of the fallen purple plums and gleaming apples. But the children were indoors, with the windows shut.

We write this book in the belief that children's lives are better spent

> in the orchard and being
> hungry and plucking
> the fruit.

O Taste and See

The world is

not with us enough,

O taste and see

The subway Bible poster said,

*meaning **The Lord**, meaning*

if anything all that lives

to the imagination's tongue,

grief, mercy, language,

tangerine, weather, to

breathe them, bite,

savor, chew, swallow, transform

into our flesh our

deaths, crossing the street, plum, quince,

living in the orchard and being

hungry and plucking

the fruit.

Denise Levertov

How to use this book

As we have already explained, this book is offered as a springboard, designed to launch educators and children into authentic exploration and enquiry into the real world from which many have been closed off too long. But it is also important to be clear what the book is not about, as well as explaining what we are trying to do. It is not a prescription for a complete curriculum, nor a framework from which to construct such a curriculum. It is not a pre-packaged set of lesson plans. It does not contain lists of learning objectives. It does not advocate that educators should take absolute control of children's lives and learning, or that they should stand back and just wait for learning to happen.

One way of explaining how the book can be used is by turning to the influential work of the early years educators in the region of Emilia Romagna, Italy. Their practices, often now referred to collectively and colloquially as the Reggio approach (after the principal city of the region, Reggio Emilia) have been recognised world-wide as having a great deal to offer other early years educators. Much of the work in their settings for children from birth to three, and from three to six, is based on what they call 'progettazione', a term which loosely translates as 'projects': cross-curricular investigations of the real world (and familiar territory to educators practising before 1988 and the structures of the National Curriculum). What is distinctive in the Reggio approach to projects is the educators' part in planning them – or rather the absence of planning as we currently think of it. They do not write short, medium or long term plans, in the English way, or work from a pre-defined curriculum of units and sub-units. But neither do they rely on chance or improvisation.

Instead they employ a process that Loris Malaguzzi, the revered champion and pioneer of the approach, calls 'reconnaissance', in which the educators embark on a 'reconnaissance flight over all the human, environmental, technical and cultural resources.' (Edwards et al 1993:85)

Each of their projects begins with a prologue phase, in which information and ideas are shared; predictions and hypotheses are made about what could happen as children bring to the project their different understandings and experiences.

> So ideas fly, bounce around, accumulate, rise up, fall apart and spread, until one of them takes a decisive hold, flies higher and conquers the whole group. Whatever it turns out to be, the adopted idea in turn adopts the children and the teachers.
> (Malaguzzi quoted in Fraser and Gestwicki 2002:176)

This is the process that this book is designed to stimulate; it is, in a sense, a companion guide to the reconnaissance or prologue phase of an enquiry, or centre of interest and study. Using this book, teachers and other educators can review some possibilities for the direction their children's enquiries might take. The key word here is possibilities: the ideas we present are only possibilities. We do not intend the suggestions we make to be used in any particular order, or to take up pre-specified periods of time. The issue of coverage has no place here: the issue of compulsion is entirely absent from our proposals. The educators who use our book, will, in consultation and negotiation with their children, make selections from our material and, more importantly, invent imaginative additions and extensions of their own.

Our intention is that by stimulating the educators' awareness of what could be done (during the children's first hand study of *Rain* or *Mysterious Objects*, for example) we will also set free some original ideas that will 'fly, bounce around, accumulate'…The educators will attentively observe which are the ideas that 'warm up' the children: 'the teachers follow the children, not the plans.' Carla Rinaldi, until recently the Director of Services to Children in Reggio, puts the same idea a different way:

> …every project is based on the attention of the educators to what

the children say and do, as well as what they do not say and do. The adults must allow enough time for the thinking and actions of the children to develop.

(Rinaldi 1998: 122-3)

We have designed the book to give educators both strength and help in working in these challenging ways; we do not offer plans, recipes or blueprints. Malaguzzi argues that the task of reconnaissance is 'to startle and push us along new roads.' We echo these aspirations.

Some of the possibilities we have suggested will be more engaging for the older children in the 3-8 age range, and some for the younger. Observant and attentive educators will respond to these differences in the interests of younger and older children by looking for opportunities to extend an enquiry or re-energise an exploration. They will also observe the moment when the children's curiosity has moved away, to another theme or focus. The educators' observations will ensure that they do not direct or determine children's enquiries, where

they could be supporting and encouraging. Observant educators will take their cues from the children. They will be aware that when adults do all the thinking and questioning, on the children's behalf, the children's commitment to the field of study will be diminished, if not extinguished. It is interesting to note, at this point, that the 2003 Welsh consultation document on the proposed new 3-7 Foundation Stage curriculum recommends very strongly that:

Young children need many more opportunities to learn through finding out about things that are of interest to them rather than focussing solely on what is determined by others.

(DTE 2003:9)

To summarise the approach we are presenting in this book, we can do no better than return to Reggio, and the words of Carla Rinaldi, who describes the work of the project approach in this memorable phrase:

a forecast of possibilities within an arena of opportunities.

Why an alphabet?
E is for everything

When I worked in a mixed-age class of five, six and seven year olds, the children loved playing with a piece of cloth with the letters of the alphabet stitched onto it, each in its own little square space. They would roll the cloth out onto the classroom floor and fetch a box of assorted objects I had collected, mostly from the insides of Christmas crackers. All these objects could be associated with several different letters. One challenge for the children was to place each object in an unexpected position: the challenge for me was to guess why. With glee they would ask me to say why the little red bus, for example, which could have been placed on 'r' or 'b' was now standing in the square marked 's'. My mind had to tune in to the logic and sharp observation of a young child, but not for the first time I was defeated. 'It's got a 73 on the front and seven starts with S!' Often they played this game in pairs so I was spared going through all the fiendish examples they thought up, but occasionally they were so pleased with what they'd done I was commanded to take a look. Thus it was that one day a child came to me after a very few minutes to announce he'd finished. Would I come and guess what he'd done? To my surprise the spaces on the alphabet cloth were all empty except the square for 'e', on which he had heaped, precariously balanced, every single object in the collection. He couldn't wait for me to speak, so pleased was he with his idea. 'Look,' he said, opening his arms expansively, 'You see, it's e! E is for everything!'

Early in our discussions of this 'First hand experience' project, we remembered this story from Annabelle Dixon's classroom and were inspired to use this child's insight as a starting point for our work. He was right: with the help of the alphabet you *can* investigate everything!

What is a first hand experience?

Using real things for a real purpose? But that is true of using coloured plastic cubes to develop a concept of number. These things are school equipment. They are real and really useful, but not what we mean in this book. We mean much more than that. We mean…

Handling and using authentic things

things that people use in the world beyond the 'school' gate. Real clay to work like a potter; seeds to plant that will grow for the real purposes of wondering, seeing, smelling and tasting; cooking for a party; making music for a concert; using wood and tools to make a rabbit hutch or a doll's house…

Going to places and meeting people

real people, real places – not necessarily a grand visit by coach, but a visit to a wood, the building site of the new estate; visits from a paramedic (complete with ambulance); a new baby; an ancient tortoise; a bee-keeper; an athlete; a chimney sweep…

Being out and about

in all weathers, day and night, running in the wind, splashing in the rain, looking at the stars, listening to the owls, crunching through frosty leaves, jumping on shadows, building a bonfire, collecting…

An extract from Aldous Huxley's last novel *Island*, first published 1962.

(Will is our hero, shipwrecked on an undiscovered paradise-type island. Mary is a schoolgirl, assigned to help look after him…)

'Believe it or not,' said Will, 'I've never seen a baby being born.'
'Never?' Mary was astonished. 'Not even when you were at school?'
'Not even at school'…
'You never saw anybody dying and you never saw anybody having a baby. How did you get to know things?'
'In the school I went to,' he said, 'we never got to know things, we only got to know words.'

These experiences are **real life experiences**. Without them children have little to draw upon in their talk and play, in their painting and drawing, in their modelling or in their story making.

They won't know at first hand the real sensations of acrid, scented, soft, soaking, bright, starlight, quiet, heavy, safe, gentle, noisy, strong, dark, enormous, tiny, cold, wet, delicious, crisp, sharp, rushing, breathless…

BOOKS

The Big Big Sea	Martin Waddell
The Storm	Kathy Henderson
The Hunter	Paul Geraghty
Susan Laughs	Jeanne Willis
In the Middle of the Night	Kathy Henderson
Yohance and the Dinosaurs	Alexis Obi

The world is not with us enough, O taste and see.

Denise Levertov

Part Two

An alphabet of learning from the real world

A is for **apple**

WHAT MATTERS TO CHILDREN what is in the world; touching and tasting the world

VISIT

an orchard
a fruit farm
the market
a supermarket
Adopt an apple tree and visit it once a month; draw it; photograph it; observe and discuss the way it changes.

MAKE

cook apples
  blackberry and apple pie
  baked apples
  toffee apples
  apple chutneys
ask parents for their recipes
plant an apple seed
plant an apple tree
make apple works of art by
  drawing
  painting
  modelling
  working on fabric...
role play stories with apples in them such as
Snow White and *The Giant's Feast*

BIG IDEAS

inner and outer, parts and wholes,
classification, naming, growth,
transformation

COLLECT

apple names – 'Worcester Pearmaine', 'Cox', 'Russet', 'Ein Shemer' (*from Thailand*), 'Benonni' (*from India*)
apples painted by various artists
  Cezanne
  Renoir
  Gauguin
  William Morris
  and artists from around the world
real apples and place them in a colour line
real apples and place them in a size line (from crab apple to 'Bramley')
apple part words
  peel
  skin
  stalk
  core
  pip
  leaf
  flesh
  wind falls
  $\frac{1}{2}, \frac{1}{4}, \frac{1}{8}$
apple products – search the supermarket shelves
apples in a variety of languages
taste apples – every possible variety

> *This is the first apple I have ever picked from a tree. I am so excited. This is wonderful. They do not grow in my country.*
> Jon, aged 39, from Iceland

BOOKS	*Johnny Appleseed*	Reeve Lindbergh
	Picture This	Alison Jay
	Snow White	Traditional
	The Tiny Seed	Eric Carle
POEMS	*Pip*	Tony Mitton
	The Apple's Song	Edwin Morgan

> *The world is not with us enough,*
> *Oh taste and see.*
> Denise Levertov

QUESTIONS WORTH ASKING

What is the difference between an apple and a tomato?
Apples are red...or are they?
Apples are this big...or are they?
Why is a crab apple called a crab apple?
How many different types of apple are there?
What is an Adam's apple?
What does, 'the apple of my eye' mean?
Why is New York called the Big Apple?
Does the tree think the apple is for eating?
Is an apple dead or alive?
How are apples used in countries around the world?

INVESTIGATE

use:
  a grater
  a knife
  a peeler
  a juicer
  a Moulinex
  a corer
how to change apples – cooking, juicing, pressing...
how apple trees grow – espalier, cordon, fan...
red apples, green apples, ripe and unripe apples, apple blossom, custard apples, fir apples, oak apples...

A is for **apple**
A learning story

The children in this story are aged four to six years in a small rural school. Just after the summer holidays one of the children, whose mother worked at the local orchard, came to school with a basket of apples. The children wrote to thank her and at their teacher's suggestion, asked if they could come to visit the orchard.

The following week, armed with clipboards, paper and grade B pencils they walked up to the orchard. The trees were laden with fruit, at child-height, and the children were intrigued by the different varieties, each with its own name. They picked apples and ate them to see which kind of apple they preferred. The bright red ones were declared the best. The children then spent the afternoon drawing the trees, individual trees and rows of trees, drawing the beehives, learning about bees and pollination, drinking the apple juice made at the orchard and buying sufficient fruit to make apple pies back at school.

The following days were apple days. The pies were made, enough for school dinners, and apple jelly. The children modelled apple shaped pots from clay. These were fired, glazed and filled with the delicious jelly.

The children learned about their locality and the contribution the orchard makes to the community; they learned that apples come from trees; that you can't have apples without bees – what a startling, unexpected fact. They learned that there are many different kinds of apple and that apples can be used in different ways: to eat raw, to cook, to make juice and jelly. They learned to look and record their observations in drawing and clay; they measured, chopped, mixed, baked and strained juice through a jelly bag; and they learned about buying and selling.

Now the children know that apples don't originate in plastic bags, weighed and sealed for the supermarket to be eaten and cooked world wide. These children have been 'living in the orchard and plucking the fruit.'

A is for **alphabets**

BIG IDEAS
communication
representation

This book is an alphabet of real experiences. Each letter can provide a springboard for children to leap into, across and through the world.

**alphabets are systems to make language visible and recorded
they look different depending on where you are in the world
China, Europe, India, Israel, Middle Earth, Russia, Middle East**

THE PEEP ALPHABET

(devised by Rosie Roberts)

In this alphabet, each letter stands for something that children would use in their schematic play – the play in which children express their pressing cognitive concerns and passionate interests – in, for example,

- up and down
- round and round
- enclosure and enveloping
- connecting
- transporting.

A – ambulance	B – ball
C – crane	D – drum
E – envelope	F – fire engine
G – gate	H – helicopter
I – insect	J – jump
K – key	L – lid
M – milk in a mug	N – necklace
O – orange	P – parcel
Q – queen	R – rain
S – suitcase, string, sandwich	T – telephone
U – umbrella	V – van
W – windmill	X – xylophone
Y – yoyo	Z – zig-zag

INVESTIGATE

codes   a range of alphabets   indexes
writing in a mirror   writing backwards
'secret' invisible writing
the eight letter musical alphabet
signing   Braille
dictionaries   address books
telephone directories
the Rosetta Stone
scripts

MAKE

- an alphabet for summer; for a festival; for a friend; for the sea; for the supermarket; of music
- a role play area of a library or a bookshop
- an illuminated letter of the alphabet
- a story written in two languages
- an alphabet of textures to be read with your fingers
- eat your way through the alphabet

SPLENDID WORDS

Runes   *Hieroglyphics*
Illuminate   *Calligraphy*

TOOLS TO WRITE WITH

pen, pencil, quill, brush,
computer and keyboard, ink, paint,
chalk, charcoal, stick

MATERIALS TO WRITE ON

paper, parchment, wall, canvas, bark,
screen, scroll, sand, leaves, rock

BOOKS

A is for Africa	Ifeoma Onyefulu
Alphabet	Alison Jay
An Abstract Alphabet	Paul Cox
Anno's Alphabet	Mitsumasa Anno
It's Now or Never	Peter Haswell
Roy Lichtenstein's ABC	Bob Adelman
The Artful Alphabet	Martina Jirankova-Limbrick

USE AN ALPHABET TO WRITE

your name
a list
a story
a message
a letter
an invitation
instructions
directions
information
a poem

QUESTIONS WORTH ASKING

Why are there different alphabets?
Why do we use an alphabet?
Why does A come first in the Latin/Roman alphabet?
Why don't all languages have 'alphabets'?

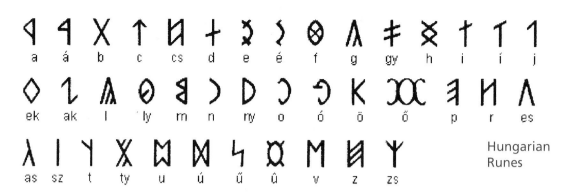

a á b c cs d e é f g gy h i í j
ek ak l ly m n ny o ó ö ő p r es
as sz t ty u ú ű û v z zs

Hungarian Runes

Greek

Dagger Script (A to F)

D -..
E .
F ..-.
G --.

J .---
K -.-
L .-..
M --

International
Morse Code

Semaphore

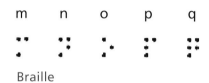

m   n   o   p   q

Braille

鼠 昌 俗 兔 龍 蛇 馬 羊 猴

Chinese

АБВГДЕЖЗИИКЛ

Cyrillic

Arabic

Uniform
Victor
Whiskey
X-ray
Yankee

Phonetic Alphabet

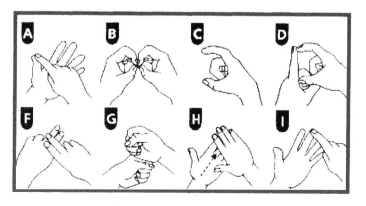

British Sign Language Finger Spelling Alphabet

שתקרצעפפ

Hebrew

A is for **alphabets**

B is for **ball**

WHAT MATTERS TO CHILDREN	moving about; having an authentic purpose; how the world works

I do not know what I may appear to the world; but to myself I seem to have been only like a boy playing on the seashore, and diverting myself in now and then finding a smoother pebble or a prettier shell than ordinary, whilst the great ocean of truth lay all undiscovered before me.

Isaac Newton

BIG IDEAS

gravity

kinetic energy

inertia

spheres and globes

QUESTIONS WORTH ASKING

Why do balls always come down when you throw them up?

Why do some balls bounce higher than others?

Is the eye really a ball?

Why are some balls hollow and some solid?

Is a raindrop a ball?

What's inside a ball?

What is 'having a ball'?

INVESTIGATE

the surfaces of bubbles

the shapes of bubbles

ball games around the world (petanque, jai-alai, hurling…)

curling up in a ball and rolling

stacking balls

the shadow of a ball

which balls bounce

how far different balls will roll

how far different balls can be thrown – try a beach ball, tennis ball, table tennis ball

the best surface to bowl a ball furthest

the balls of the feet – travel on them

the surface of a golf ball

playing football with a golf ball

playing tennis with a beach ball

bouncing a ball off a pillow

making your favourite ball go faster/slower

how to kick or throw a curve ball

MAKE

balls of clay from tiniest to largest – and join to make…?
a hollow clay moon
snowballs
balls of hessian fibres
soap bubbles
a new ball game
mobiles of planets

Look at the forged ball bearing sculptures of Antony Gormley

Bodies in Space 1, 11, 111,1V and V (2001)

Standing Matter 1, 11, and 111 (2001)

www.antonygormley.com

COLLECT

balls for sports and games
sort by: size, surface, weight, density
sort bats in the same way and match them with the balls

LOOK AT

demolition ball
crystal ball
star gazing ball
peas in a pod
frogspawn
ball and socket joints
ball on a tow bar
ball-bearings
the inside of a cricket ball
moon
hedgehogs
woodlice
marbles
alliums (onion family) and dandelion seed heads
rabbit droppings
puffballs
seeds we eat (peppercorns, coriander)

ORDER

best rollers
bouncers
best for throwing
catching
spinning
kicking
batting
bowling

VISIT

Shakespeare's Globe Theatre
a cricket ball maker
any athlete who uses a ball
a bowling alley
a bowling green
observatories

BOOKS

Careful With That Ball, Eugene!	Tohby Riddle
Pickle and the Ball	Lynn Breeze
Sometimes I Like to Curl Up in a Ball	Vicki Churchill
The Monster Who Ate My Peas	Danny Schnitzlein
Winnie Plays Ball	Leda Schubert

B is for **brushes**

COLLECT

look in the kitchen
bottlebrush, scrubbing brush, dustpan and brush, vacuum cleaner, pastry brush

use all these brushes

look out of doors
besom, cow's tail, grooming horses and dogs, street cleaners, carwash, a fox's tail, ostrich feathers

look in the bedroom and bathroom
nailbrush, toothbrush, mascara, hairbrush, nail varnish brush

look in stories
broomsticks!

VISIT

a car wash
a train wash
a riding stable
an artist's studio
the caretaker's cupboard
a cabinet maker
a jazz band
a curling team
a chimney sweep
and more…

provide a mystery brush – speculate

I wonder how many different hairbrushes there are…

Van Gogh must have used a very fat brush for this bit.

don't forget to ask children's parents – they will want to contribute

BIG IDEAS

causality: means-end

fitness for purpose

identity and difference

transformation and reversibility

classification

Let's put all the ones with handles together.

MUSIC
The Sorcerer's Apprentice

You can't sweep a yard with a toothbrush.

The clean dishes don't stay clean.

*W*atch (children's) interest… listen to their questions… then you will not be able to doubt the strength and spontaneity of their wish to know and understand.
Susan Isaacs

MAKE

a mascara brush for a giant
a carwash for Noddy's car
a nailbrush for an elephant
a hairbrush for a lion

QUESTIONS WORTH ASKING

What makes a brush a brush?
Is a teasel a brush? Or a hedgehog? Or a doormat?
What's the difference between a brush and a comb?
Why are there so many different brushes?
Are there some things you CAN'T brush?
If you haven't got a brush, what can you use?
(see also questions worth asking about bags)

BOOKS

Cinderella	Traditional
Hair	Gerald Rose
Meg and Mog	Helen Nicholl and Jan Pienkowski

LIST

the functions of brushes

cleaning
polishing
smoothing
adding
covering
playing the drums…

B is for bags

BIG IDEAS

variety

diversity

scale

form and function
(the necessary relation)

transporting

inside and outside

materials

---

collect, classify*, search the world, search your mind, compare

discuss fitness for purpose

express this relationship in talk; in play**; in modelling; in drawing (the necessary relation)

observe the world

real problem solving – finding the right bag for the job

cooking: samosas, ravioli, Cornish pasties, empanadas

collecting, naming, classifying*

PRECIOUS BAGS
a doctor's bag   a princess's bag   moneybags   a wallet

*CLASSIFY
by function – satchel, rucksack, sleeping bag, tea-bag
by owner – postman, doctor, hiker, cricketer
by fastening – button, zip, string, velcro
by materials – velvet, leather, plastic, paper
by country of origin – raw materials or place of manufacture

---

make a sleeping bag for a teddy
make a bag for an umbrella

A fishing net is a good bag for carrying fish, but not so good for carrying water!

*W*e hold that children's understanding is better fostered by meeting their natural interests in the world as a whole, and using their spontaneous impulses to handle and explore, than by giving set lessons in history, geography and the 3 R's.

Susan Isaacs

** PLAY
the educator's part in play:
- provide a variety of bags for play
- organise opportunities to play bag stories
- document the narratives of play

(Mary Jane Drummond, 1996)

...fantasy play is the glue that binds together all other pursuits, including the early teaching of reading and writing skills...

Vivian Gussin Paley

QUESTIONS WORTH ASKING

What makes a bag a bag?

Is a sack a bag?

Is a tea strainer a bag? Is a suitcase? An envelope? A scabbard?

Who uses bags? Why?

What would a witch's bag look like? Or a giant's?

Are some bags baskets? Or some baskets bags?

What can't you put in a bag?

VISIT

Royal Mail sorting office

a sleeping bag factory

a handbag shop

a leather workshop

the museum

BOOKS

Don't Forget the Bacon	Pat Hutchins
Handa's Surprise	Eileen Browne
My Granny's Purse	Paul Hanson
The Lighthouse Keeper's Lunch	Ronda and David Armitage
The Mitten	Jan Brett
The Paper Bag Princess	Robert Munsch

Focus on learning

B is for brushes and bags: these two pages explore very similar possibilities, with common themes and conceptual form.

The educator's task is to organise and stimulate enquiry, engagement and detailed discussion of the collections that the children create (with encouragement and support from you and the children's families), and the observations they make of real things being used in the real world.

The children's work is to search the world for variety and diversity: their discoveries will lead them to understand how this fragment of the world works – as long as they have plenty of time to talk about the big ideas they encounter and to represent them in a variety of ways, in their talk, in their play, in their dance and music making, in their drawings, models and paintings.

Working with bags and brushes will **strengthen children's powers**
• to do (notice, observe, record, use tools, collect, search)
• to think (classify, compare, analyse, predict, reason, justify)
• to understand (form and function, diversity, causality, reversibility)
• to represent and express (in talk, in models, in construction, in play, in movement, in music and sound).

Working with bags and brushes will **extend children's learning** As they work they will learn what the world is made of – not just in terms of *things* and the materials things are made of – but in terms of *ideas*. The ideas they will learn about are important ones, with a necessary part to play in the children's full-time project of meaning making. At the same time they will be learning about themselves, and their powers to ask questions, explore ideas, to debate and discuss, to speculate, to imagine new possibilities.

Making connections

In the course of exploring the possibilities outlined on these two pages, there are interesting connections that could be made with other letters of the alphabet, especially
• C is for collections
• F is for furniture
• M is for mysterious objects
We hope that every page of this book will stimulate rewarding, sometimes unexpected connections of these kinds. (see also the Z is for zig-zag pages)

C is for **collections**

| | |

WHAT MATTERS TO CHILDREN   touching things; having an authentic purpose; acting on the world; knowing the world; making my world map; a sense of big belonging

shells, buttons, gemstones, pebbles, badges, ribbons, cards, superheroes, erasers, postcards, pencils, books, hats, rubber bands, stamps…what is missing?

COLLECTIVE NOUNS swan, herd, flock, gaggle, clutch, brood, flight, crowd, cluster, team, army, congregation, school, litter, quartet, orchestra…

BIG IDEAS
sorting and classifying
inclusion   exclusion
order   pattern

VISIT

a concert: *what is on the programme? Is the music a collection by one composer? Is there a choir?*

an art gallery: *find a collection about a theme such as stories, big events, food, special people, journeys. Paint your own picture to fit with the collection.*

a museum: *what collections have been made by other people – fans, armour, trains? How can you arrange your own collection?*

a library: *borrow a collection of books about…castles, frogs, giants, pirates, owls…or by the same author.*

a nursery: *choose a collection of plants and explain why they go together.*

MAKE A COLLECTION OF WORDS
wet words
dark words
small words
blue words – navy, turquoise, sky, royal, Delft
guinea pig words

PATTERNS ARE MADE WITH COLLECTIONS

- natural objects – *look at the environmental sculptures of Andy Goldsworthy and Richard Long*
- made objects – *buttons, pom-poms, keys, wing nuts, screws…*
- printmaking tools
- mark making tools – *look at the painting 'Lines of Marks' by Wassily Kandinsky*
- numbers sounds, dance sequences

MAKE A COLLECTION OF PATTERNS
Rangoli, Kente cloth, Australian Aboriginal paintings…

MAKE A LIST
shopping
things to do
holiday packing
names for my baby
places to visit
favourite stories

LOOK AT A PAINTING OF A COLLECTION
My Gems   William Harnett
Letter Rack   John Peto
make a painting or drawing of your own collection

BOOKS
A Four-Tongued Alphabet   Ruth Brown
Anno's Mysterious Multiplying Jar
    Mitsumasa and Masaichiro Anno
I-Spy Animals in Art   Lucy Micklethwait
The Willow Pattern Story   Alan Drummond
POEMS
A Child's Book of Lullabies   Shona McKellar
Skip Across the Ocean   Floella Benjamin

BOOKS OF COLLECTIONS
alphabets
dictionaries
photograph albums
counting books
phone books
crossword puzzles
recipes
postcards
short stories
poetry anthologies
musical pieces
make your own

QUESTIONS WORTH ASKING
How many make a collection?
Is everything part of a collection?
Is there anything that does not belong to a collection?
What is the opposite of a collection?
How many people make a crowd?

Children are full time researchers, untiring remakers of actions, ideas and theories.
Loris Malaguzzi

COLLECTIONS OF PEOPLE
crowd, party, class, school, congregation, choir, nation

THINK ABOUT
separate, unique, alone, individual, isolated, single

C is for **collections**

Using books as a springboard

> The following is a collection of books. Each book could be a springboard into exploration and discovery or could enrich children's growing understanding of difficult and important ideas and experience. These books can also deepen an understanding already within the child's framework of experience.

A is for **apple**
The Giant's Feast by Max Bolliger
The tale of two giants, the smaller of whom outwits all older and bigger giants at the annual feast.

A is for **alphabets**
The Blue and Green Planet by Brian Patten
The earth is the ark gradually accumulating creatures and features of the planet in alphabetical order.

B is for **ball**
Seven Ways to Catch the Moon by Mark Robertson
The magic number seven - seven wishes, seven magpies, seven parts of a tangram…

B is for **bags**
Crocodile Crocodile by Peter Nickl
The rights of crocodiles and all creatures with valuable skin.

B is for **brushes**
Room on the Broom by Julia Donaldson
The ultimate good witch story in which broom rhymes with room and resolution is achieved through caring and sharing and working together.

C is for **collections**
Frog and Toad Make a List by Arnold Lobel
For all compulsive list makers: those who need to order, sort, arrange, plan, categorise, organise.

D is for **doors**
The Lion, the Witch and the Wardrobe by C.S. Lewis
Four children enter a world of adventure and self-discovery when they open the wardrobe door.
An abridged version beautifully illustrated by Christian Burningham is available.

E is for **enemies**
Where the Wild Things Are by Maurice Sendak
Max is wildly testing the world, but even he, despite his intrepid nature, chooses to leave the land of the wild things and return to where someone loves him best of all.

F is for **furniture**
Peepo! by Janet and Allan Ahlberg
Enchanting illustrations of life at home during the second world war. Spot the differences between then and now.

G is for green

The Green Ship by Quentin Blake
Sailing from the reality of a ship-shaped topiary into the world of imagination until the players all grow too old for this game and the tree becomes itself again.

H is for homes

The Colour of Home by Mary Hoffman
Hassan, who had to leave his home, Somalia, to live in England likes to paint and when he goes to his new school he starts to paint a picture of his home: the blue sky, the yellow sun and all his familyand the animals where he used to live. But…

I is for 'I'

The Boy and the Cloth of Dreams by Jenny Koralek
Silver threads from the moon and golden threads from the sun are needed to mend the tear in James's quilt. To fetch these threads he has to journey through the house at night to face his fear of the dark and to 'forge his own courage'.

J is for joining

The Little Boat by Kathy Henderson
A little boat made of polystyrene, string and a stick travels across the world from one child to another.

K is for knowing

Tree of Crtes by Allen Say
Knowing your roots and who you are. This story is a new slant on Christmas through the eyes of a Japanese child, with the crane as a symbol of peace.

L is for looking

Chidi Only Likes Blue: an African Book of Colours by Ifeoma Onyefulu
Chidi's sister Nneka introduces him to the rich world of colour they live in, but still Chidi only likes blue.

M is for mixing

The Great Blueness by Arnold Lobel
A wizard who lives at the time of the great greyness mixes new magic which he calls 'blue'. As the villagers grow tired of blue, the patient wizard mixes yellow, then red. But what can you do when there are no more primary colours to mix?

M is for mysterious objects

Fossil Girl by Catherine Brighton
Mary Anning, the child who discovered the ichthyosaur, adds it to her mother's collection of 'curiosities'.

N is for nothing

Nothing by Mick Inkpen
How do you feel when you are called 'Nothing'? Luckily someone who values him and even remembers his name and the time when he was somebody special finds Nothing.

O is for opposites

Elephant Elements by Francisco Pittau and Bernadette Gervais
Elephants on every page depicting opposing attributes – broken, mended; full, empty; hairy, smooth.

P is for physical

Frog by Susan Cooper
In which we learn about the nature of human beings and frogs and in which Joe learns to swim 'just like Frog'.

Q is for questions

Why do the Stars Come Out at Night? by Annalena McAfee
Imaginative responses to a child's quest for knowledge.

R is for **rain**

The Water Hole by Graeme Base
The animals gather round an ever-diminishing water hole until they are faced with the prospect of extinction. Then it rains. This is an exquisite book.

S is for **surfaces**

Where the Forest Meets the Sea by Jeannie Baker
Illustrated by collages that are a tactile experience in themselves, this story reflects on the beauty of the natural world and leads us to think of a future under a concrete jungle.

T is for **Tate** and other **galleries**

Camille and the Sunflowers by Laurence Anholt
Vincent Van Gogh shows his appreciation of his welcome to Arles by painting portraits of Camille and his family

U is for **under**

Amazing Anthony Ant by Lorna and Graham Philpot
Under the ground is a maze where Anthony Ant lives his exciting life. Clues to his exploits are hidden under the flaps.

V is for **variety**

The Creation Story by Norman Messenger
The wealth and diversity of life on this planet retold by the artistry of Norman Messenger.

W is for **windows**

Window by Jeannie Baker
A story without words. Look through the window and notice the changes as the years go by.

X marks the **spot**

Once Upon an Every Day by Toby Forward
A child dreams of the unattainable but realises the value and joy of everyday life.

Y is for **yesterday**

Wilfrid Gordon MacDonald Partridge by Mem Fox
A child grapples with the notion of memory – an abstract concept given meaning by his experience of the real world.

Z is for **zig-zag**

Big Band by Barbara Nascimbeni
A real zig-zag book to use as a starting point for making music.

D is for **doors**

MAKE

a witch's fridge

a mouse's bungalow

a Bedouin tent...

QUESTIONS WORTH ASKING

Is a gate a door?

Is a letter box a door?

Has a suitcase got a door?

Why don't kennels have doors?

What makes a door a door?

VERBS

observe **d**esign **m**ake

saw **g**lue **m**odel

buy (hinges, handles, glue)

photograph **d**raw **a**sk questions

FIND ANIMAL DOORS

beehive

mouse hole

whelk

cat flap

bird cage

COUNT

doors in the kitchen – cooker, fridge, cabinets

the numbers on doors

BOOKS

Doors	Roxie Munro
Sara and the Door	Virginia Jensen
The Rain Door	Russell Hoban
The Sign on Rosie's Door	Maurice Sendak
Who's at the Door?	Jonathan Allen

POEMS

The Door	Miroslav Holub

MATERIALS

glass doors

curtains

garage doors

the office safe

zip doors on a tent

fly screens

INVESTIGATE

the parts of doors...

hinges

handles

latches

keyholes

eyepieces

bolts

locks

keys

buttons (on a lift)

doors in the street

phone box

letter box

cat flaps

If a yurt has no door, how can you get in?

Does everything that opens also shut?

Does every room have a door?

Does every house have a front door?

Every question is a door handle.
George MacDonald

COLLECT
other things that open and shut
inkwells; umbrellas; suitcases...

BIG IDEAS
diversity
form and function
fitness for purpose
human ingenuity
the familiar is fascinating

VISIT
the biggest door – cathedral? guildhall? temple? shopping mall? fire station?
a joiner's workshop
the oldest door
the smallest door – where is it?

DISCUSS METAPHORS
An eyelid is a door to the eye.
The lips are a door to...

Dis for **doors**

A learning story

I work with children in a Foundation Stage unit consisting of a nursery, where three and four year old children attend in two groups for half a day each day, and a class of four and five year olds. The reception class runs along the same lines as the nursery with play based learning and a regular time for a sit down snack.

Our planned topic for the half term was 'Buildings' so the pages 'D is for doors' and 'H is for houses' fitted in and worked well together.

Before getting started, I familiarised myself with the major themes of the book. I tried to get to grips with 'what matters to children' as fully as I could. I internalised the 'questions worth asking' for 'D is for doors'. I think this really helped me because that way I had the questions ready as prompts, if the right time to use them with children should come up.

I didn't plan anything. I wanted to follow the children's interests and see what happened. It meant a lot of close observing and real listening. In fact, within the larger umbrella theme of our topic on buildings, the children didn't spontaneously pursue any investigation of doors. I was disappointed, but going back to the text, I decided to set up a display with 'door furniture' such as locks, handles and hinges. On reflection, there seemed to be more hinges on display than anything. I don't know if this was the reason, but interest in door hinges, and hinges everywhere really took off. I was amazed at the children's responses. Amy commented on the hinges saying,

'You get those on windows and on doors.' So I asked, 'Can a window be a door?'

Amy hypothesized at great length about windows operating as doors. Beth concluded that 'They both let fresh air in and ladybirds too.' (We had found a ladybird walking about earlier). She elaborated that we wouldn't need doors if windows came in different sizes for different people and if they could be at different heights. She said that babies needed windows they could roll out of to explore the world, and she mimed top-hinged swinging windows. She obviously saw doors as a problem for babies and their explorations, unlike adults who more often see them as a solution! Her thoughts led to further considerations about how rooms could be built with various different windows for different people.

I drew the group's attention to the hinges on display. Amy again became very interested, focusing on the smallest hinge in the collection, from a jewel box. She said, 'This must have come from a fairy's door. I don't know what has happened to her'. She held on to the hinge for ages, describing what the fairy looked like and that she lived in the bottom of a tree. The hinge inspired her story and her play.

Carly recognised one hinge in the display as the same type as the one on the door to the toilet. We all went to investigate this, which led to the group wanting to look for hinges all around them. This was not something I had thought of and after sorting out support staff to look after the remaining children, we decided to go on a hinge hunt and we took cameras to capture the images.

I was really surprised when the children's first stop was in the classroom at the book box. Delia pulled out a book and declared, 'Look! **This opens and shuts like a hinge.**' They proceeded to find so many other hinged things — swing bin lids, high level door closers, hinges on easels, window hinges. I was really struck by how much interest they had in hinges. For several consecutive days after, the children brought in hinges or told me of somewhere else they had found them.

The children posed a lot of questions for themselves and were encouraged to explore their own thoughts. For example:

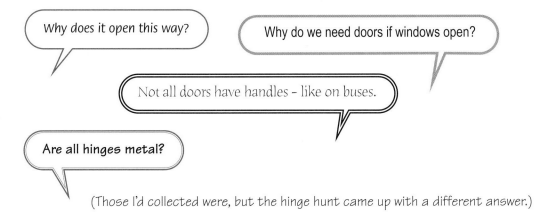

Why does it open this way?

Why do we need doors if windows open?

Not all doors have handles - like on buses.

Are all hinges metal?

(Those I'd collected were, but the hinge hunt came up with a different answer.)

The Big Ideas section for 'D is for doors', says 'The familiar is fascinating.' This was certainly so in this case. The experience confirmed for me that the simplest things can be of real interest to children and that many adults who work with and care for children so easily forget this, in our rushed familiar world. We easily forget what it is like to be discovering, perhaps for the first time, something that is right under our noses.

Other things I could have done

I could so easily have let the children run with the idea much further and I am convinced their activities would have covered so many areas of learning.

I tried to scribe the fairy's story, but should have recorded it at the time.

I would love to have sent a camera home for the children to have photographed a door to talk about and will do so next time.

I regret not arranging a small delegation to investigate bus doors. Do all buses have doors? Do any bus doors have handles? It would have been possible, at least, for a small supervised group to travel on a bus from one stop to the next one and then take a return journey to report their findings and inspire new questions. Visits don't have to be grand and involve everyone.

We could have gone beyond the school to investigate.

The children's learning

It was quite apparent that the children were engaged in higher levels of thinking. Their genuine interest promoted higher order questioning quite naturally, without me having to plan sessions to cover this. They were more committed, more focused and more interested in what they were doing. All the children kept really busy and stuck at what they were doing. Their interest in door (and other) hinges spanned a range of investigations: gravity, weather, the properties of shapes and the needs of babies. Even their play and story telling were affected by this project.

My learning

This project supports my view that, compared to adults, children can have equally interesting, sometimes better ideas, theories and hypotheses about things in the world. They are much more interested in finding the answers to their own lines of enquiry than in any enquiries I suggest to them. I had decided to follow their lead and although at times it was hard to hold back from a direction I wanted them to follow, it was worth it. I really think that the hinge hunt will remain a multi-sensory memory for the group of children involved – they still talk about hinges.

E is for enemies

WHAT MATTERS TO CHILDREN
being with friends; moral maps; me and the rest of the world; who is in the world? who am I in the world?

INVESTIGATE
Do animals have enemies?
Places where enemies go
Where do enemies come from?
Have I got an enemy?
Am I an enemy?
Can enemies be nice?

VERBS
loving
hating
caring
fighting
breaking
destroying
crying
dying
rescuing
controlling
befriending
attacking
worrying

QUESTIONS WORTH ASKING
What makes an enemy? Do enemies have friends? Does Tyrannosaurus Rex have any friends? How do you get to become an enemy? Am I an enemy? Is it okay to be friends with an enemy? How do enemies make you feel? How do enemies feel? If you are friends with an enemy, does that make you bad? Are enemies always enemies? What do enemies look like? Where do enemies live? Does everyone have enemies? Does everything have enemies? Do ALL animals have enemies? Are hunters good people? Are enemies bad?

MAKE
a place safe from enemies

a place where enemies are

a place where enemies play together

MUSIC
Heroes and Villains Brian Wilson
Purple People Eater Sheb Wooley
Romeo and Juliet Prokoviev
Star Wars John Williams
The Monster Mash Bobby Boris Pickett
1812 Overture Tchaikovsky

OPPOSITES
love	hate
caring	destruction
safety	danger
friend	enemy
rage	reconciliation
power	powerless
leader	victim
control	controlled
defend	attack
attack	liberate
Superman	Weedyman
goodies	baddies
heroes	villains
enemies	friends
terrorist	peacemaker
prejudice	acceptance

Everyone is your friend until you find out they are not.
George, aged 5

VISIT
an aquarium with sharks
the zoo
a spider's web
a war memorial
a cemetery

TOOLS
role play materials
blocks, planks and blankets for making dens and camps
superhero capes
the outdoor world
mini world
superheroes
the natural world

Children are the most implacable enemies of boredom.
Loris Malaguzzi

BIG IDEAS
power and control
good and bad
death
destruction
loneliness
love
friendship
caring
equality
discrimination

Let the boys be robbers, then, or tough guys in space. It is the natural, universal and essential play of little boys.
Vivian Gussin Paley

BOOKS
Best of Friends Shaun and Sally Anne Lambert
Cops and Robbers Janet and Allen Ahlberg
I Want To Be a Cowgirl Tony Ross and Jeanne Willis
Monster Poems John Foster and Korky Paul
Pumpkin Soup Helen Cooper
The Hunter Paul Geraghty

Children expect the help and truthfulness of grown-ups. Loris Malaguzzi

BOOKS FOR EDUCATORS
The Kindness of Children Vivian Gussin Paley
Boys and Girls: Superheroes in the Doll Corner Vivian Gussin Paley
The Genius of Play Sally Jenkinson
Combating Discrimination: Persona Dolls in Action Babette Brown

E is for **enemies**
Learning stories

Many educators report that although children pursue this theme independently in many different ways, it is rarely expanded and supported as an area of investigation. But when educators looked more closely at the play and questions of children, they saw that children are powerful thinkers when it comes to this theme. Some children are more excited and motivated to learn than their educators had ever noticed before. The examples below illustrate a variety of starting points.

Starting point 1

I work with four and five year old children, and recently a new girl, Sonia, joined my reception class. When she arrived she went straight to the sand tray and played with all the plastic animals, quite violently. And then in the water tray too the animals all fought, under her control.

At the end of the day I talked with her mother. She told me that there were problems at home, lots of arguments and grievances constantly in the air. Routines and stable relationships had been turned upside down. She said they'd been let down by loved ones. The family didn't know who to trust and turn to. It seemed that Sonia was exploring relationships and conflicts, asking, 'What is an enemy?' in her play.

Starting point 2

Another educator, also working with four and five year olds, reflected on how work on this theme had begun.

It all started in the run up to last year's Remembrance Day, when I'd heard a reception child ask, 'Why do we have to buy the poppies?' I was intrigued by the responses from the children.

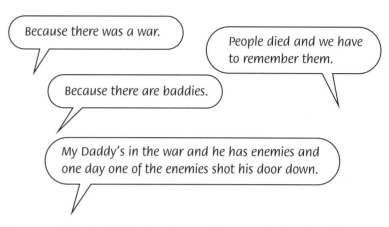

Then one child asked, "Do the Germans buy poppies too?" and our work on enemies could not be halted.

Starting point 3

Parents in one infant school had been asked to watch their children playing at home and became involved in the themes of their play. One parent had gone as far as writing notes on her son's play. She talked to the class teacher about it.

Vasos is always playing with dinosaurs and toys he gets from his older cousins. He loves anything really gruesome. I noticed he was playing with the plastic dinosaurs (again) and also had by him a plastic skeleton hand filled with tiny plastic ghosts and ghouls. He was talking as he played and then he started to tell me: 'These (ghosts) are the baddies. They are all baddies because they are ghosts and all ghosts are bad and they don't have any friends except other ghosts. And here is tyrannosaurus and he is really bad. He is the enemy of all the dinosaurs because he eats them. He is a carnivore and he can only have another tyrannosaurus for his friends. But if he wants to fight the other tyrannosaurus, he won't be their friend and then he is the enemy of everyone. But that's sad. So maybe he has just one special T. Rex friend. Maybe…

…But if you ever see a tyrannosaurus, and you can't because they are extinct, except there is one in the museum only its not real, even though it can roar…if you ever saw one, you couldn't really be its friend. You would just have to hide. That's what I would do. No use trying to be its friend. You can't. YOU CAN'T BE FRIENDS WITH TYRANNOSAURUS.

I don't think you would be its enemy. And you wouldn't be a baddie. You would just have to hide. The only enemy a T.Rex has is another T.Rex. If they are not friends. Not you. You are too weak.
It might have enemies of ghosts. Yeah. Maybe that's it. Because I think all the ghosts are bad. And they would scare T.Rex.'

The mother's story of her son's play was the trigger for the educator to work on themes that were in tune with the questions Vasos was asking as a player.

Starting point 4
In another setting an educator was watching children engaged in small world play. She noted that as they played they reflected on enemies and revealed their thinking about:

What an enemy is; what enemies do; how you get to become an enemy; who an is enemy and how you can stop being one; how to be safe from enemies.

Talk from the small world play session

Jamie	Their [enemies'] mummy doesn't teach them to be good. I'm an enemy of someone, but my mummy's teaching me not to be. Everyone's an enemy of someone. Jack is my enemy, he attacks me…
Kiran	The enemy is attacking your goodie.
Lenny	This one's fighting the tyrannosaurus.
Mike	The T.Rex is an enemy because he's got sharp teeth. He's trying to make the enemy dead. The elephant will run away from him…If you have two enemies they'll be friends. They fight Spiderman.
Orest	He's a baddie, he's got a scary face…
Pablo	If you whack a baddie you might change into a baddie. A baddie might change into an even more baddie.
Quentin	I've made a cage for the dog in case he flies away because he's got wings.
Orest	That's his castle and he's trying to kill my baddie and he can't that's why I put him in my castle.
Ruby	To keep safe from a baddie you can run away.
Shakila	I am making a safe place for my cat in a house.
Pablo	He's not an enemy because he's a person…well some enemies aren't persons and some are.
Quentin	…If a goodie hits a baddie then he gets [to be] a baddie.
Orest	Yes, and if a baddie hits a baddie then he gets a worse baddie.
Pablo	T.Rex are enemies because they're meat eaters. It was fighting because it wanted to make him dead and eat him.
Orest	You can't eat him because he's got dangerous teeth.
Quentin	Simon's my enemy. But I'm sad because he's not at school today. He wasn't in assembly and he wasn't at lunch. So we can't play enemies.
Tammy	…He's bad. He's got sharp teeth.
Ute	White shoes means a good guy.
Ruby	On our video the goodie had silver shoes.

Kiran	Sharks are sometimes good when you touch them. That guy looks like evil because he has red eyes.
Ute	I'm going to build a wall [to keep my goody safe from baddies].
Quentin	Sharks can kill people.
Kiran	Yeah but when there's a rough sea there was a great white shark who was biting a fisherman's leg. But the fisherman had a boot on and the shark didn't even hurt him.
Ute	It's got a gate.
Kiran	The Incredible Hulk doesn't need a safe place because he's too strong to have a safe place.
Ute	These are bad ones. They want to get him but they won't get him because the gates are locked…They've climbed over the gate.
Kiran	Ute, that goody should attack the baddie because goodies do attack.
Quentin	It's got breathing fire out of its mouth. It's a good dragon. It fights baddies so that they're dead.
Ute	They've made a monster tent. No, they're not baddies any more. Because they're happy.
	(Ute has piled all the bricks she can find in a mound on top of her superhero.)
Quentin	Ute – they can still get in. They can still kill him.
Ute	They can't – 'cos he's locked in the maze – no – 'cos there's a big cage inside – no way!
Kiran	He's got locked in there because he's naughty. They're all baddies 'cos they are wicked.
Quentin	…There aren't real baddies, 'cos they've all got killed…

The children spontaneously played enemies in their small world play and other kinds of play, both indoors and outdoors. They drew pictures of enemies and talked about this as they drew. They listened to stories featuring friends who fall out, such as **Pumpkin Soup** and re-enacted these in group activities, in role play and using small world story boxes.

The educator said 'I was amazed that one sheet of paper on enemies could have produced enough work to last me for at least a term. The enemies project…replaced the week when I was going to investigate "friends", and was infinitely more exciting.'

F is for **furniture**

WHAT MATTERS TO CHILDREN   touching things; exploring how they work

Never forget...
The child's interest in the concrete events of the physical world.

Susan Isaacs

INVESTIGATE

furniture in kitchens
fridge
toaster
balti dish
chapatti roller
wok
mincing machine
salad spinner

furniture in bedrooms
cots and baby beds
bunk beds
camp beds
hammocks
four poster
futon

discuss

> My husband falls asleep in the bath.

> My friend's baby slept in a chest of drawers.

chairs
folding
revolving
fixed and portable
(shooting stick)
a milking stool
a nursing chair
a dentist's chair
wheelchairs
Van Gogh's chair

tables
their number of legs
– 4, 1, 3, 0?
their purpose –
altar, airline tray,
desk, board room
their workings –
flaps, extension
leaves
their shapes

COLLECT AND FIND

collect pictures of
tables
beds
chairs
mirrors
stairs
find
the biggest
the smallest
the oldest
the newest
the easiest to make
the most beautiful

BIG IDEAS

form and function
fitness for purpose
(real purpose)
adaptability
substitutes
diversity

VISIT

factories
a church
studios
a museum
a banqueting hall
a narrow boat
a gurdwara

VERBS

collect
discuss
visit
draw
design and make
polish
compare and
contrast
deconstruct
reassemble
evaluate
plane
decorate
stain
model
reduce and
enlarge

CONNECTIONS

D is for doors
H is for homes
W is for windows

MATERIALS

What is furniture made of?
Why? Why not?
Is it
old or new?
precious or cheap?
hand made or mass produced?
decorated or plain?
shiny or soft?
outdoors or indoors?

QUESTIONS WORTH ASKING

Why are there so many different ways of making a bed, a chair, a table?
Why do cats and dogs have beds but not chairs or tables?
What would you do if you didn't have any furniture?

MAKE

design and make furniture for
  kings and queens
  a giant
  a baby
  a doll's house…
make the bed for the princess
in The Princess and the Pea

VIDEO

L'enfant et les Sortilèges
Nederlans Dans Theater,
Choreographer, Jiri Kylan
www.euronet.nl/users/cardi/Videos.html

DISCUSS

many different kinds of furniture
  mirrors
  clocks
  stairs – garden, library, steps
  fixed and moveable - ladders,
  fire escapes, rope ladders…
substitutes:
if you haven't got a clock use a…
if you haven't got a ladder use a…

BOOKS

Billy Tibbles Moves Out! Jan Fearnley
The Princess and the Pea Traditional
The Three Bears Traditional
Six Dinner Sid Inga Moore
The Magic Bed John Burningham
What! Kate Lum and Adrian Johnson

Children, like poets, writers, musicians and scientists, are avid seekers and builders of images. Loris Malaguzzi

F is for **furniture**

A learning story

In a small one-class entry infant school in a large industrial city, the staff entered on a month long investigation of furniture. Each class took a different theme, focusing on a different aspect of this enormous topic.

The reception class

To enrich the very young children's domestic play, the educators in this class embarked on an investigation of launderette furniture. Some children had been playing with bubbles in the water tray. One child remarked, 'It's like a washing machine.' Another ran to the book box and found a story book with launderette washing machines on the front cover, called *The Frogs go on Holiday*. The children asked the teacher to read it aloud to them and when she did, one asked, 'Is there really such a thing as launderettes?' The very next day a small group set off to find out. They returned delighted with the proclamation, 'Launderettes are really, really real and they have LOADS of good things in them.' But what exactly? The next day another small group set off to investigate, 'What do launderettes have in them?' They returned bursting with, 'Machines...machines is what they have. All different ones. Washing machines, spinning machines, drying machines, money change machines, washing powder machines, big bag machines in case you've lost your big bag.'

While other delegations visited the launderette throughout the week to find out about launderette life, the remaining children set about recreating a launderette world by making launderette furniture. Within less than a week the corridor outside this part of the school (the class shared two large adjoining rooms) was transformed. A long row of washers and driers, created from a fine collection of cardboard boxes, stood on one side, and on the other, a row of chairs labelled with the name and logo of this flourishing establishment. They played launderettes in their newly created role play area. At most times of the day a group of mothers and fathers, with their babies in buggies, could be found sitting in the launderette, gossiping about their children's illnesses, the price of soap, the length of the wash cycle, or reading magazines and making shopping lists as they waited for their load to finish. Service washes were available and dry cleaning was taken in. Two busy employees checked in loads of washing, ticking off items and estimating prices and delivery times. There was often a great drama about a missing sock or shirt. When monsters or robbers appeared, they usually brought a bag of washing with them to put through a wash cycle, waiting patiently as true launderette customers do, before resuming their monster or robber behaviour.

The rest of the school was organised into four parallel mixed age classes of five, six and seven year olds. The teachers consulted each other and decided on different approaches to the common enquiry, basing their choices on children's current interests and selecting a different curricular focus from their most recent whole class enquiry.

Class 1

This class of children were deeply into traditional fairy tales and so The Three Bears' house was set up. The construction work was challenging. The task of building two chairs that would hold the children's weight and a third that would collapse to order, proved almost endlessly demanding, but was eventually mastered by the children. The beds were easier, thanks to Community Playthings.

The kitchen furniture was no problem, and then the cooking could begin. The head teacher recorded in her log, ruefully, that she had NEVER eaten so much porridge.

On some days bears could be seen in the launderette, bringing a bag of washing to do while the porridge cooled down.

Class 2

Here the focus was on folding furniture. Day after day parents arrived at the classroom door with deck chairs, high chairs, camp beds, shooting sticks, camping tables and chairs, buggies, card tables, step ladders and more, much more. These objects were investigated, drawn and labelled and their working explained. Then the

model making began, at first with art straws. But the children were soon dissatisfied with folding furniture that didn't fold properly. More problem solving. More attentive study of the deck chairs – the favourite items in the collection (despite the squeezed fingers and sticking plasters).

Class 3

This was taught by two part- time teachers. They planned an enquiry into office furniture. One of them led the factual side of the project and small groups of children visited the school office to explore the mysteries of filing cabinets, word processors, revolving chairs, photocopiers and answer phones. They completed inventories and interviewed the office staff. They measured the time it took to word process a letter on the computer and the time it took to write one by hand. They discussed the reason for each item of

furniture being in the office, and in the course of the discussion, worked on the big ideas of fitness for purpose and the relationship between form and function. They debated the question, 'What makes an office an office?' and concluded that it wasn't the furniture: what makes an office is the things that people do there.

The second teacher took charge of recreating an office in the classroom as a stimulus for office play. The children were especially delighted by the arrival in their classroom of a tall metal cabinet containing some wire clothes hangers and a broken umbrella…all kinds of stories resulted and the cabinet was soon full of clothes to match the characters in these stories. This part of the work culminated in the public performance of an office drama, scripted by the children, in two parts, though this was not at first announced. In the first part a stereotyped female secretary (meek, polite, and undemanding) was bullied by an equally stereotyped male boss (three piece pin striped suit). Before the head teacher could leap to her feet to point out the evils of this representation, (the whole school were working on an equity awareness project) the second part of the drama began and the two roles were reversed! The moral lesson became plain, especially to the humbled and contrite head teacher.

Class 4

The class chose to investigate one aspect of kitchen furniture, the fridge. There were many expeditions to the fridge in the school cooking area, to take temperatures, to collect ice cubes for experiment and re-experiment. They spent a long time researching this interesting question: how many times will the same piece of ice melt and re-freeze? This enquiry was curtailed by the weary teacher after thirteen repeats. She urged the children to move on. A lost opportunity perhaps?

The fridge in the school kitchen was explored, measured, drawn and labelled, its contents inventoried and the school cook interviewed.

The resourceful class teacher discovered a site in the city's industrial zone where discarded refrigerators were stored before being destroyed. She collected two specimens, one large and one small and brought them into the classroom. Children of course were instructed about the dangers of actually going inside a fridge. Much purposeful activity followed, as every constituent part of them was investigated, compared, contrasted and discussed. To conclude the project, the logic of things gave way to the logic of the imagination (see T is for thinking) and the children filled the refrigerators with 3D models of appropriate food: for a giant in the large fridge, and food for a witch in the small one. The green and slimy potions that filled the witch's fridge were unforgettable. Some of the parents were amused but not complacent. 'Wherever have the children seen such loathsome little green dishes before?' they wondered.

G is for **green**

> **WHAT MATTERS TO CHILDREN**   being with living things; being in authentic places; what the world is made of

VISIT
Christmas tree plantation
botanic gardens
nature reserves
farms, farmers' markets
greenhouses and potting sheds
nurseries
community gardens and allotments
arboretum
green maze
The Eden Project
The Lost Gardens of Heligan

BOOKS
Dinosaurs and All That Rubbish
Michael Foreman

Linnea in Monet's Garden
Cristina Bjork

The Global Garden
Kate Petty and Jennie Maizels

The Selfish Giant
Oscar Wilde

The Very Hungry Caterpillar
Eric Carle

POEMS
Green Man Lane
Tony Mitton

Overheard on a Saltmarsh
Harold Munro

Pied Beauty
Gerard Manley Hopkins

QUESTIONS WORTH ASKING
When can you eat green?
Can you eat plants?
Where does the soil come from?
How deep in the ground does green grow?
How does green feel?
Are ALL green things plants?
Are there any green roots?

FIND
where these green animals live:
dragonflies, grasshoppers
caterpillars, leaf hoppers
aphids, frogs
the smallest plants – and the largest/tallest
the smallest seed and largest seed
green woodpeckers, greenfinches
the Green Man
all the different names for green: viridian, emerald, olive, speckled frog

COLLECT
plants you can eat
the smallest plants
a list of plants in the grounds from moss to giant oaks
leaves of different shapes – including cabbage, pak choi, chives, banana, and water lilies…

BIG IDEAS
recycling
food from the sun
transformation
change

MAKE
a garden the size of a shoe box
a green man
a garden chair
a garden for wildlife
a green maze
a wormery
an area to grow plants
a compost heap
a menu for an aphid's restaurant
a paddy field
paint environments where animals are camouflaged

BIG WORDS
photosynthesis
chlorophyll
etiolated
ecology
ecosystem

INVESTIGATE
what happens when you put a plant in the cupboard for a week but still water it?

how to make it better when it comes out

where the green goes in winter

what happens to plants when they die

is all of the plant green?

what do birds, butterflies and bees like?

mixing green paint from blue and yellow

as many greens you can mix – and give them all a name

green rocks

common names and scientific names

algae

evergreens

green lights

We should be conscious of the scale of the child's world – often of most importance to the child is what is possible for him or her to hold in a cupped hand.
Schools Council

G is for green

A learning story

Our class of vertically grouped seven to nine year olds from an urban school visited a botanical garden just before Easter. On arrival we learned how old the garden was, and where many of the plants had come from in the world. ('When was the first flower planted?')

We listened to the Oscar Wilde fairy tale, *The Selfish Giant*, about small children who enjoyed playing in the giant's fabulous garden while he was away. When he returns, he banishes the children by building a wall and putting up a sign 'Trespassers Will Be Prosecuted'. ('That means beheaded!') The garden becomes so unhappy that winter settles and stays permanently. Snow, frost, wind and hail ('Hail is water frozen…you can tell it's hail 'cos it bounces.') lash the garden. The situation is resolved by the appearance of a very special child, who softens the giant's heart so that he relents and allows the children back into the garden and spring and summer return.

We made a giant's garden in clay, using a range of carefully structured exploratory, yet imaginative techniques. ('It smells lovely and when it gets mould on it, it turns into mushrooms.') Having created trees, shrubs, ponds, and streams, they were quickly drawn into the construction of their own imaginary gardens, and suggested all kinds of features – sheds, wheelbarrows, vegetable plots, hedgehogs, tools, all of which demanded the application of techniques learned in the initial exploration and transferred to new inventions. They were quick to modify and adapt the techniques to invent their own features: cylinders could represent sturdy tree trunks, limbs, worms and coiled snails; plaiting them could form streams; rolling one end more than the other formed cones that could be carrots, or giant aroids, or hedgehog spines. 'You could do loads of flowers and a stalk and then join them all together!' enthused one child, while another adapted techniques to create a hideous monster. Each child's garden acquired new and marvellous features as the work went on: bridges, bird fountains and banana trees sprang up with speed and were shared around the class, inspiring others. Some forms were so imaginative as to be as yet unknown to science, although we still hadn't seen what the botanical garden had to offer.

Given the children's interest this activity could have lasted an entire day, but we broke for a quick lunch and then set off to explore the garden, taking bags to collect treasures lying on the ground.

We found a quiet spot and closed our eyes and listened: we heard birdsong, water in the fountain, children's voices and the wind in the trees. At another spot we just used our eyes: ripples on the water in the pool, dead leaves under the boxwood hedges, a feather, pine needles, grass, gravel, clouds, bark and leaves. We walked on to another place to inhale the intense smells from fragrant early flowering shrubs like osmanthus, viburnum, and mahonia. At another we stroked the needles of a pine tree as long as the hair of an old English sheepdog, felt the bristles of the cones and trod on the spongy carpet of pine needle litter beneath the conifers.

We had been advised that there were no giants in *this* garden, but we found a giant sequoia tree nearly 62 metres tall, with moss – one of the smallest plants – growing on its bark. We collected many intriguing treasures that had fallen from the plants: cones, needles, dried leaves ('Why are some of the leaves all crispy?') and seed pods. On returning indoors, we listened to a poem about the Green Man; we looked at pictures and carvings of green men sprouting leaves from their faces, but also green cats, lions and snakes, from churches and cathedrals. The children sorted their treasures and selected favourites, ranging from pods, bamboo stalks, turquoise petals, sequoia cones and furry magnolia bud scales like wing cases - if ladybirds could be the size of mice.

We gave children large rectangles of loosely woven jute, with which to make Green Man masks. Red dogwood stems from the garden were provided to weave across the top to hang the piece, while threads were extracted across the bottom to create long loose threads – a beard which the children could knot or plait, as they chose. The extracted threads were tied back in at the top to make hair, while some were saved for moustaches. Eyes and a mouth were easily suggested by pulling the threads apart in the appropriate places. Moss, dried leaves, seed heads, evergreens and cones were woven and tied into the mask, highlighted by their treasures, ('Cool! Look at the texture of it!'). The children worked quickly and again, this activity could have lasted an entire day, but after an hour we had to leave and so took our masks and treasure bags with us to finish back at school. All of the treasures were gradually incorporated through weaving and tying and were hung against windows and walls, where they provide a fragrant reminder of our visit and a stimulus to further collecting in our own environment.

H is for homes

WHAT MATTERS TO CHILDREN   belonging; well-being; keeping safe

HOMES MADE BY PEOPLE
- aquarium
- hutch
- coop
- stable
- house
- trailer
- caravan
- bungalow
- flat
- byre
- hive
- safari park
- barracks
- monastery
- igloo
- manyatta
- castle
- tepee
- prison
- hospital
- dovecot
- tent
- palace
- kennel
- cage
- Bedouin tent
- narrow boat

HOMES NOT MADE BY PEOPLE
- nest
- shell
- burrow
- lair
- den
- dray
- web
- anthill
- sett
- cocoon

HABITATS
- pond
- river
- swamp
- hedgerow
- fen
- marsh
- moor
- coral reef
- trees
- field
- rain forest
- sea
- soil

QUESTIONS WORTH ASKING
Is there anywhere that is not a home? What if your home was a castle, a cave, a houseboat or a tent? What if you had no home? Where do you *not* want to live?

DO
make a tree house, a crooked house, a den
look at spider's webs
investigate a bird's nest
make clay bricks
build a cruck frame house
grow plants in a green house
collect and sort pictures of homes

HOME BORROWERS
hermit crab
cuckoo
ghosts

VISIT
- hothouse
- greenhouse
- lighthouse
- henhouse
- tree house
- Mansion House
- penthouse
- houseboat
- butterfly house
- warehouse
- caravan

HOMES IN ART
Victorian Interior Pippin
Japanese Interior Toyaharu
Tar Beach II Ringgold
The Bedroom Van Gogh

BIG IDEAS
diversity, fitness for purpose, shelter and protection, safety and comfort, survival and luxury

Children need access to a place where they can dig in the earth, build huts and dens with timber, take really great risks and learn to overcome them. They want a place where they can create and destroy, where they can build their own worlds, with their own skills, at their own time and in their own way.
Lady Allen of Hurtwood

BOOKS
Hansel and Gretel	Jane Ray
The Mousehole Cat	Antonia Barber
Three Little Pigs	Traditional

POEMS
Colonel Fazackerley	Charles Causley
The Blue Room	Richard Edwards
The Key to the Kingdom	Traditional
The Listeners	Walter de la Mare

H is for **homes**

Learning stories

I work in a Foundation Stage unit for children from three to five. Our topic for the half term was buildings, so 'H is for homes' and 'D is for doors', were good starting points for our enquiries. As with doors, I didn't plan anything. I wanted to follow the children's interests and see what happened. I knew this might be difficult, but I was determined to stick with it and let the children lead the way for me. This approach to teaching means a lot more close observation and real listening in its widest sense.

Initially we talked about where we live and what we live in. There is a variety of housing in the area and a range of different buildings too. Simply walking around, not far from the school, gave us lots of scope to see and compare the buildings in the neighbourhood. On one occasion children photographed different types of buildings which provoked plenty of discussion back at school. The walk had taken them past some houses which were under construction. This led to their decision to set up their own building site, in both the outdoor and indoor areas because building takes place indoors and outdoors, as the children pointed out. We have had building sites set up for play and investigation in the past. Several parents are builders or keen DIY enthusiasts and because of this real materials are not a problem to collect. The building site evolved over the week. Children realized they could not reproduce a whole brick house so they embarked on creating their own structures. Some used breeze blocks and set about inventing a recipe for good cement. Others used blocks and planks to make den style houses, rather than brick based.

All their building involved negotiating and planning things for themselves: they used adults as sounding boards for their ideas. There were no problems with safety issues as children rarely seem to set themselves challenges beyond the limits of safety.

A group of children began to construct a den. One boy looked at it and remarked, 'That's not a real house. It's a play house.' Children agreed that play houses didn't have roofs but real houses did. It seemed quite obvious that they would want to turn their den into a real house by adding a roof. So, undaunted by the difficulties ahead, the children collaborated on this task. There was much discussion about safety and the need for roof supports. Hard hats were called for. They collaborated and worked hard to agree on a way of putting up a roof support and building a safe roof. I was redundant. I merely observed and learned so much about the children. I was thrilled to see the children stick with the problem and staying focused. The roof issue remained a major area of interest. Outdoor walks now meant looking at roof constructions. We studied roof tiles and made our own in clay. As their interest continued, they started to make dens, with cloths over tables and chairs. They went on to build homes from various recyclable materials.

I have never let them take their own enquiry and activity quite that far before. My own pre-planned objectives were covered early and much more easily. They seemed to be doing it all for me! It was as if they'd done all my planning and identified the learning objectives I had to cover. My role was simply to observe and support without intruding. I didn't ask the 'questions worth asking' unless the moment was just right. Then I'd just drop them in, to take their thinking on. I let the children go in the direction they wanted to. The whole experience confirmed for me that children should play a much larger part in deciding what they do.

In future I'd like to base my own plans on what matters to children. I want to continue to involve them much more. If I work with older children, six or seven year olds next year, I'll definitely work in exactly the same way.

In a small group in a class of five and six year olds, one boy asked a question totally unrelated to the activity they were engaged in, 'Is a spider's web a home?'

The educator said nothing, but waited to see how the children in the group would answer. At first they seemed to ignore his question, but came up with Spiderman related comments.

'Spiderman makes webs.'

'He shoots them like this' [making Spiderman actions].

'Yeah he catches all the baddies. He traps them in his webs.'

The boy who had asked the original question came back with, 'Yeah, but I'VE seen a REAL spider's web AND A REAL spider was making it.'

'But Spiderman makes real webs too.'

'No. Only spiders. Spiderman's not real, so how can he make real webs?'

'Well he DOES. And spiders don't. It's only Spiderman who can make webs…(he pondered) DO spiders make webs? DO they?'

'They do, I watched one in my house, but I don't know if they actually live in their webs, so are spider's webs homes?'

'But how do they make the webs? Do they shoot them out like Spiderman? HOW do they do it?'

The teacher asked, 'Simon, have you ever seen a real spider's web?'

'A REAL spider's web? A Spiderman's web? In my video Spiderman makes the webs.'

There were now clearly two things to investigate. The next steps were obvious.

 is for 'I' the active learner at the heart of education

This page is the first of six pages that are rather different in format. The others are K for knowing, L for listening and looking, Q for questions, T for thinking and Z for zig-zag. On this page we expand on some of the thinking that lies behind the whole book and that underpins our argument: young children need active, first hand experiences to feed and exercise their growing human powers.

The problem as we see it

- loss of time, space, autonomy
- take-over by educators who do children's thinking and doing for them
- proliferation of second-hand experiences – paper and pencil, internet, video and computer images

The alternative

- reinstate children as powerful agents in their own learning
- reinstate children's access to the real, meaningful, living world
- reactivate children's capacity to act for themselves

I AM

From birth children tell us of their essential being…
'I AM, I FEEL, I SUFFER, I LOVE, I REACH OUT, I TOUCH, I EXPLORE, I EXPERIMENT, I MAKE MEANING'.

'I AM' becomes 'I CAN'

As children grow so do their powers to act on the world…
I CAN…touch it, taste it, prod it, eat it, adapt it
I CAN collect bits of it
I CAN share it with my friends
I CAN ask questions about it
I CAN make connections between different bits of it
I CAN tell you which bits fascinate me
I CAN talk about all these things I do.

AND SO I LEARN

to know bits of the world
to know what they mean
to understand bit by bit the places and people and things and feelings that make up my world.

WHAT MATTERS TO CHILDREN

From birth, children know what's important to them. This book takes 'what matters to children' as the basis for proposing ways in which their fascination with the world can be encouraged, extended and deepened.

IT'S IMPORTANT TO ME!

what is in the world
who is in the world
touching and tasting the world
knowing the world
making sense of the world
exploring how things work
moving about in the world
acting on the world, making a mark on it
being engaged, with authentic purposes
being with friends
being in different kinds of places
making collections
having a sense of big belonging
making my own world map and moral map
finding out what the world is made of
being in the world of living things
understanding how the world works
finding out how to keep safe in the world.

I is for 'I' the active learner at the heart of education

The view of children as active learners that we are putting forward on these pages is not a new invention. Classic texts about children, schools and learning are full of powerful expressions of this very theme; contemporary writers continue to emphasise the same idea.

> The child who is learning by doing is learning many things besides the one thing he is supposed to be learning. He is learning to desire, to purpose, to place, to initiate, to execute: he is learning to profit by experience, to think, to reason, to judge.
>
> Edmond Holmes

No sticks or carrots needed…

> Rather than asking 'What stick or carrot will make the children active in certain ways?' or 'what will make them go in this direction rather than that?' we would do well to turn the problem round and to say: children will go in any case, for it is an expression of their being to be purposeful and energetic…
>
> R. A. Hodgkin

> In order to be creative, a child needs not only the opportunity but also the capacity, the power to make a choice.
>
> Christian Schiller

> Children have valuable contributions to make to the present and the future. We should value their contributions and let them grow.
>
> An educator who participated in the development of this book

> It is not what we do to the child or for the child that educates him, but what we enable him to do for himself, to see and learn and feel and understand for himself. The child grows by his own efforts and his own real experience.
>
> Susan Isaacs

> (We have) a highly optimistic view of the child; a child who possesses many resources at birth, and with an extraordinary potential which has never ceased to amaze us; a child with the independent means to build up his or her own thoughts, ideas, questions and attempts at answers; with a high level of competence in conversing with adults, the capacity to observe things and reconstruct them in their entirety. This is a gifted child, for whom we need a gifted teacher.
>
> Loris Malaguzzi

J is for *joining*

WHAT MATTERS TO CHILDREN — touching things; what the world's made of; how the world works

QUESTIONS WORTH ASKING

Why do some joins move and some not?

If it's been joined together can it be un-joined? Sometimes? Always? Never?

Who uses joins and joining in their work?

Why is some writing joined up?

Are some things too big to join – or too small?

How do people join things without nails? Or glue? Or tools?

When human beings join together, what do they make? A team? A party? A band? A meeting? A demonstration? A war? A club? A union?

COLLECT

paper clips
string
nails and screws
elastic bands
crochet hooks
buttons
zips
pins
glue
sellotape
duct tape
screw drivers
hammer
pliers
chains

MAKE

daisy chain
human chain
books
jigsaws
a box with a hinge
a railway with junctions
lei

BIG IDEAS

form and function

diversity

fitness for purpose

INVESTIGATE

a skeleton
a skull
a bicycle
pair of scissors
an estuary
the horizon
how many joins in a door? a book?
how many hinges in a room? a street?
find some things with no joins in them
unravel some knitting
patchwork

> You can know the name of a bird in all the languages of the world, but when you're finished, you'll know absolutely nothing whatever about the bird…So let's look at the bird and see what it's doing – that's what counts. I learned very early the difference between knowing the name of something and knowing something.
>
> Richard Feynman

OBSERVE

how doors join onto walls
how sleeves join onto jackets
how fingers join onto hands
how feathers join onto birds
how pages join into a book
how hands join together

VISIT

a joiner at work
a dressmaker at work
a railway junction
sketch
photograph
observe
interview
document
make music

USE

all of the above for useful projects

DECIDE

what's the most effective joining material and joining tool?

DISCUSS

Some useful joins and joints (legs, holding hands, a bicycle chain).

All the different ways of joining clothes… which is the best?

BOOKS

A Most Unusual Lunch	Robert Bender
Little Cloud	Eric Carle
Over The Steamy Swamp	Paul Geraghty
The Great Big Enormous Turnip	Alexei Tolstoy
The Peach Tree	Norman Pike

J is for joining
A learning story

An early years unit used a range of approaches to explore the properties of joining. Their planning reflected the way in which the educators at this unit matched 'First Hand Experience: what matters to children' with the Foundation Stage early learning goals. On the weekly planning sheet the educators identified key learning objectives. These were matched to first hand experiences that would enrich the learning selected from the page J is for joining.

A physical approach

The children linked their bodies in movement sessions, twisting, rolling, and making arches, climbing under and over linked hands to make different patterns. They also used parachute games to develop their awareness of space and to work cooperatively with others.

In the construction area the children joined wood and card using a range of tools and techniques to investigate fixed, moveable and hinged joints.
The children built car and railway tracks and a variety of forms of transport using large cardboard boxes linked together using string, rope or card, and towers from construction kits. In this way the children learned to compare sizes, to name shapes and to consider investigative questions such as,
> Which building wobbles the most?
> Why do you think this is?
> How does this joint work?
> Would these joins work with cardboard boxes?

They learned through first hand experience the meaning of joint, hinge, strong, fixed, moveable, arch, stretch, flexible, rigid, transport, push and pull.

Outdoors, in the rain, the children played with gutters supported on boxes to send plastic ducks down the tubes. They explored questions like:
> Did the ducks travel more quickly than the cars?
> Is water a better means of transport than wheels?
> How long can we make the chute and does it make a difference?

The story of *The Enormous Turnip* was read and retold by the children using story box characters. The children made their own books to write their versions of the story, learning ways to join pages and chapters together, and using joining words such as 'then', 'next', 'later', 'afterwards' and 'but'.

At the end of the enquiry the educators looked back at their planning sheets and were surprised and delighted at the unexpected and valuable learning that had taken place. The achievements of the children surpassed the early learning goals identified on the planning sheets. The learning had been richer, deeper and completely engaging.

K is for knowing

On these pages we offer some suggestions about the kinds of knowing that matter most to children. We have become very familiar with long lists of the things children are expected to know and understand at certain ages. We recognise the importance of this kind of knowing in children's development. The relation of letters to sounds, the conventions of written English, the vocabulary of addition and subtraction: of course all this knowledge is important. But there are other kinds of knowing that are just as significant for children's intellectual development, especially:

KNOWING HOW

KNOWING WHERE

KNOWING WHEN

KNOWING WHO

and KNOWING WHY

WHAT MATTERS TO CHILDREN

In these kinds of knowing, children are learning to understand more about the questions that most concern them: questions about the world and their place in it, the place of other people in their world, how the world works and how people behave.

BOOKS

A Ladder to the Stars	Simon Puttock
Drop Dead!	Babette Cole
Goodbye Mog	Judith Kerr
Supposing	Frances Thomas and Ross Collins
Tell Me Again About the Night I was Born	Jamie Lee Curtis

Children are always ready to shake the tree of knowledge.
Loris Malaguzzi

Be a confident unknower.
Guy Claxton

Since we cannot know what knowledge will be most needed in the future, it is senseless to try to teach it in advance. Instead we should try to turn out people who love learning so much and who learn so well that they will learn whatever needs to be learned.

John Holt

KNOWING HOW
How did the world begin?
How do I know who my friends are?
How do my fingernails grow?

KNOWING WHERE
Where do my dreams come from?
Where was I when I wasn't here?
Where can I go in the world?
Where do people go when they die?

KNOWING WHEN
When will it be yesterday again?
When am I safe?
When will the world end?

KNOWING WHO
Who is in charge of the world?
Who am I?
Who is the tooth fairy?

KNOWING WHY
Why am I here?
Why am I me?
Why are things unfair?
Is there a reason for everything?

Q is for questions
There is more to read about children's questions on the page 'Q is for questions'. The questions on this page are just reminders of the kinds of knowing that matter most to children; they are not intended as suggestions for questions that adults could or should expect all children to answer! And besides, we have to remember that different children know – and want to know – different things.

BIG IDEAS

As children explore these questions and many others like them, they are working on the life long project of understanding some very big ideas indeed, for example: CAUSE and EFFECT, TIME, MYSTERY, IDENTITY, RECIPROCITY, MORAL RESPONSIBILITY, LIFE and DEATH.

(In the nursery school) the children are free to explore and experiment with the physical world, the way things are made, the fashion in which they break and burn, the properties of water and gas and electric light, the rain, the sunshine, the wind and the frost. The teacher is there to (bring) together the material and the situations which may give children the means of answering their own questions about the world.

Susan Isaacs

The power (and limits) of reason

In arguing that it is important for children to think about the 'why' questions that most concern them, we do not want to suggest that every 'why' question can be answered with a completely satisfactory and reasonable answer. The power of reason is both enormous and limited.

Which of us can answer 'why' questions about earthquakes, avalanches or car accidents? Or say why some things move us to tears of joy? Or why we find some parts of our world incomparably beautiful? Some problems cannot be answered by the power of reason.

Children have the capacity to turn to the logic of the imagination, when the logic of the rational world doesn't seem to apply.

(Also look on the pages for T is for thinking)

L is for **listening and looking**

On this page we argue that every first hand activity engaged in by children involves looking and listening of some kind, sometimes many kinds. The educator's responsibility is to make sure the conditions are totally supportive of worthwhile looking and listening. The most important thing to remember is that worthwhile looking and listening take time. None of us can look or listen properly if we are being hurried. We need plenty of time for these simple ways of making sense of our experience, and, what's more, we need plenty of time to talk about what we see and hear. Children's looking and listening are no different, but they depend on their educators to provide the time and the space they require.

[Bissex] emphasises, as I have tried to do...the vital importance of listening, watching and waiting, if we are to have any hope of supporting and extending children's learning. In her unforgettable words:
We speak of starting with a child 'where he is', which in one sense is not to assert an educational desideratum but an intangible fact: there is no other place the child can start from. There are only other places the teacher can start from.

Bissex 1980:111

Observing children is simply the best way there is of knowing where they are, where they have been and where they will go next.

(Mary Jane Drummond 1998)

Worthwhile looking means:

taking it slowly

talking about what you see

looking again and again

looking at details

looking for surprises

looking for what is missing

talking about what you see

looking and comparing

looking near and looking far

looking at everything

looking at one thing at a time

looking at new things, animals, plants

looking at mysterious things

talking about what you see

looking at the real thing, not an image of it

looking at beauty

looking at pain

looking at turbulence

looking at harmony

looking with your hands as well as your eyes

Worthwhile listening means:

taking it slowly

asking questions, not just answering them

listening to your friends

listening to yourself

listening to everybody's ideas

listening to everybody's stories

listening to their discoveries

listening to their meanings

listening to difference

listening to agreement

listening to debate and discussion

listening to objections

listening to complaints

talking about what you hear – not the sounds, but the meanings

listening with an open heart

All children, including those who are blind and deaf, use all the senses they have for looking and listening.

AN EXAMPLE FROM THE CLASSROOM

Child: Do our moon moth caterpillars have claws or toe nails?

Teacher: I'm really not sure.

Child: Can I find out? I need to look at it very hard.

[focused looking for 90 mins]

Teacher: What have you found out?

Child: I still can't decide. It's really difficult. It could be one or the other.

Reference books provided no further clues, merely general reference to pseudopods, but a letter to a Professor at the University of Aberystwyth provided the answer:

TOENAILS

It was accompanied by the comment that in all his experience only one other student had ever tried to answer this question – and certainly no six year old child.

The Chinese character for listening is made up of four different characters all of which are involved in the work of listening.

EAR	EYE
BRAIN	HEART

EXAMPLES IN THIS BOOK

A is for apples: visit an apple tree once a month for a year

Q is for questions: use a question book

M is for mysterious objects: make a collection of objects both familiar and unfamiliar

PRACTICAL SUGGESTIONS FOR EDUCATORS

Use the technique that Reggio educators call 're-presentation'; document children's talk while you are listening and looking together. Later, use your notes of their talk to identify ideas and comments you would like to explore and extend. 'Re-present' these ideas and comments to the children, inviting them to say more, to debate with each other and with you, to take their thinking and learning to a deeper level.

Provide plenty of magnifiers of different kinds, and keep readily available. A microscope is invaluable, especially for older children.

Take children's talk seriously (see also T is for thinking).

BOOKS FOR EDUCATORS

Assessing Children's Learning	Mary Jane Drummond
Assessment in Early Childhood Settings: Learning Stories	Margaret Carr
The Genius of Play	Sally Jenkinson
Listening to Four Year Olds	Jacqui Cousins
Listening to Young Children: the Mosaic Approach	Alison Clarke and Peter Moss
Dialogues with Children	Gareth Matthews

M is for mixing

Where drawing may be the string quartet of art, the richness of painting is nearer to being a symphony.

Rob Barnes

BOOKS

A Million Chameleons   James Young
In the Night Kitchen   Maurice Sendak
Pretend Soup: and Other Real Recipes
          Mollie Katzen and Ann Henderson
The Giant Jam Sandwich John Vernon Lord
The Mixed up Chameleon   Eric Carle
The Magnificent I Can Read Music Book
          Kate Petty and Jenny Maizels
make a role play area for any of these books

LOOK FOR WELL KNOWN MIXES
rainbow hundreds and thousands
sweet and sour   guitar and harmonica
the dawn chorus   fish and chips
bricks and mortar   rice and peas
Rama and Sita...

QUESTIONS WORTH ASKING
Does everything change when it is mixed with something else?
What mixtures can you un-mix? bread? fruit salad?
portmanteau words? cement? clay?
How can you un-mix sounds?

USE
blender
mincer
whisk
fork
spoon
palette knife
spatula
brush
tape recorder
sound mixer
cocktail shaker
compost maker
loom
spirtle
ice-cream maker
pestle and mortar
taps
filters and sieves
hands
cement mixer

MIXING PEOPLE
a class of children
friends
a community
a football team
a continent
a world
a family

BIG IDEAS
identifying
naming
classifying
combining
adding
change

VISIT
a recording studio
a concert
an art gallery
a garden
a kitchen
a bakery
a building site

THINK ABOUT THESE WORDS
mixture, combination, collection, pollution

INVESTIGATE

mixing with water
teabags, shampoo, dried fruit, coffee, paint, soil

mixing sounds
sounds that are alike
sounds that are different
instruments that make quiet, loud, sudden, continuous sounds
combining sounds to make music that makes you think of the sea, a storm, wind, rain
singing different sounds at the same time – round
mud and compost

mixing smells
flower perfume
a cocktail of smells made from water, leaves, grass, flowers, soil, other natural materials

INVESTIGATE

mixing colour
mixing paint
twisting yarns for weaving, stitching, making tapestry
overlaying cellophane, net, tissue paper
dyeing cloth, batik, tie and dye
blending pastels; crayons

mixing flavours
breads – naan, pitta, chapatti;
biscuits;
cakes; jams; jellies; drinks; soups;
sandwiches; curries; muesli; teas

magic spells
a spell to make you blue
a spell to make you happy
a spell to make you small

LIST
compound words (two whole words in one)
skyscraper, suitcase, snowflake, armchair, birthday, Superman, handkerchief, rainbow, weekend
portmanteau words (two part words in one)
chocoholic, brunch, motel, guestimate, mimsy, slithy
colour mixture words
purple, orange, brown, beige, green, turquoise, pink, mauve, grey

M is for **mixing**

Learning story one

The following investigation was planned for my class of children aged four to six years.

It was one of four mini projects within the 'mixing' theme – mixing garden cocktails, mixing paint, mixing food, investigating things that don't mix.

I allocated an afternoon for each mini project over the space of a week, with a view to adapting my planning to respond to the children's interests.

Mixing garden cocktails

As a whole class, we talked about mixing smells from the garden in our outdoor area. To investigate further, we went on a class walk around the school grounds to collect suitable things we could add to our cocktails. The children found materials such as leaves, grass, petals and soil.

I provided some water and jars. The children then selected the natural objects they wanted to mix together and spent over an hour mixing up their cocktails. Some children revised their ideas as they were going along, by removing and then adding various things until their cocktail was just right. Most children gave their mixture a name and they enjoyed smelling each other's cocktails.

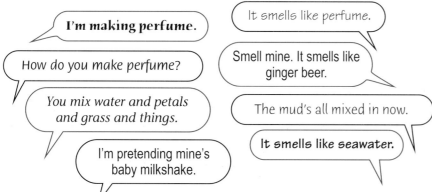

I'm making perfume.

How do you make perfume?

You mix water and petals and grass and things.

I'm pretending mine's baby milkshake.

It smells like perfume.

Smell mine. It smells like ginger beer.

The mud's all mixed in now.

It smells like seawater.

Learning story two

In a nursery classroom Simon sat alone at a table. He'd come in from outside where he had just been looking at the pond and asking about frogs.

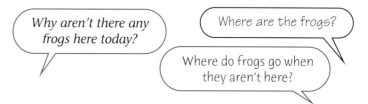

Why aren't there any frogs here today?

Where are the frogs?

Where do frogs go when they aren't here?

He remembered that he'd got a frog picture in a book and went inside to find it, but instead he started to gather tools for mixing powder paint. He got a palette and spoon, and some white, yellow and blue paint. He spooned a little white paint into the palette and looked at it. He spooned some yellow paint on top of the white and reached for a brush. He mixed the yellow and white powder together. He looked at the new pale yellow. He added a tiny amount of blue. He mixed it. He looked at the mixture and smiled and then continued in this way with the blue paint for some time. He then reached for more yellow, loading the powder onto the spoon. As his arm hovered above the new green mix, he faltered and some yellow powder floated down, making tiny spots on the green. He paused and looked delighted, studying the paint for some time, before shouting out to everyone triumphantly,

I've done it, I've done it. I've made speckled frog green. AND IT'S A REALLY *GOOD* ONE TOO!

M is for mysterious objects

WHAT MATTERS TO CHILDREN   how the world works; things the world is made of

WHY INVESTIGATE OBJECTS?
There are things you can learn from an object that you cannot learn from a secondary source like a photograph. The most commonplace object can reveal so much information if we learn to ask the right questions of it.

VISIT
places with unusual objects: museums a castle places of worship a factory an historic house a sculpture park a garage a restaurant kitchen

BIG IDEAS
classifying
sorting
diversity
everything has a purpose

INVESTIGATE
a mysterious object is some thing unfamiliar to the children, some thing they do not recognise – a spaghetti spoon, a hot water bottle stopper, a chapatti rolling pin…

ask children:
  What do you know for certain about the object?
  What do you think you know?
  What questions could you ask to help you find out more? (any question except, 'What is it?')

pictures which look different when upside down or highly magnified

Objects have a remarkable capacity to motivate. They develop the 'need to know' which will spark children's interests, then their curiosity or creativity, and then stimulate their research. Handling objects is a form of active learning that engages children in a way other methods often fail to do.
Gail Durbin, Susan Morris, Sue Wilkinson

MAKE
- a themed museum about a place, a person or a time
- put a mysterious object in a feely bag and guess what it is from someone else's description
- play Kim's Game (recalling objects on a tray) but instead of just recalling the hidden objects classify them according to different categories e.g. objects made from metal, objects found in the kitchen…
- make a drawing of an object from memory then from observation
- fill a suitcase or a bag with objects belonging to a person – real or imaginary and ask the children to work out who it belongs to
- mysterious objects of the future – someone volunteers 'to die' and lies down to be buried with their favourite possessions – what will remain in one month, 200 years?

THINK AND TALK ABOUT
What does it look and feel like?
  What is it made of?
  Is it made from natural materials or manufactured?
  Is the object whole?
  What colour is it?
  What size is it?
How is it made?
  Is it made by hand or machine or both?
  How has it been put together?
  Was it made in one or more pieces?
What was it made for?
  How is it used?
  Is it still used in the same way?
Why does it look the way it does?
  Is it decorated? If so how?
  Do you like the look of it? Does everybody think the same?
  Does it work well? Does it do the job it was designed for?

BOOKS
Five Children and It
  E Nesbit
Frank in Time
  Rod Clement
If at First You Do Not See
  Ruth Brown
The Copper Tin Cup
  Carole Lexa Schaefer
The Lost Thing
  Shaun Tan
The Sandal
  Tony Bradman

COLLECT
objects (both familiar and unfamiliar)
organise and classify the objects according to:
  their place of origin
  how they are made
  how they are designed and decorated
  the materials from which they are made
  their age
  their function
make a time line
make themed collections – mysterious musical instruments, kitchen utensils, garden tools, writing implements…

QUESTIONS WORTH ASKING
What makes an object mysterious, unusual, interesting…?
Is a mysterious object mysterious to everyone?
Can a picture, painting or poem be a mysterious object?
Does every object have a purpose?

M is for mysterious objects

Learning stories

As a teacher, I believe that observation of an object is very important. Children need to be able to make observations about an object before they can go on to make deductions, ask questions and form hypotheses.

Learning story one

A class of 19 four and five year old children sat in a circle on the carpet and passed round an unfamiliar object. They had not only to observe the object closely, but listen to each other and try to say something about the mysterious object that no one else had said.

'It's got a bird on it.'

'I can see a plant.'

'It's got a hole in it.'

'It's got a handle.'

'I can see some berries.'

'The thing is hard.'

'And it's round.'

'There's a stripe.'…

The children made 19 different statements.
The mysterious object was a ceramic egg separator.

Learning story two

Assumptions

A class of five and six year old children were sitting back to back, one holding a familiar object. The objects were household objects, a plug, a toothbrush, a screwdriver, a candle for example. The aim of the activity was for the children without the object, to guess what their partner was holding by asking questions – What is it made of? What size is it? In which room of the house would it be found? And so on.

A puzzled partner asked for help. 'Ryan has told me its size and that it is round, black and white and made of rubber and plastic, but he doesn't know which room you would find it in, or how it works. What is it?'

The children were helped and told that the most likely place to find this object would be in a bedroom. Ryan's partner still looked puzzled and said, 'I still don't know what it is. What is it?'

To put the children at their ease they were told that they were handling a hot water bottle stopper. The quick reply came in unison, 'What's a hot water bottle?'

One person's familiar object is another person's mysterious object. (See also the U is for under learning story.)

Can I bring in an object for the rest of the class to guess?

Questions asked about a chapatti rolling pin

'Do you hit things with it?'   'Is it used for making music?'

'Is it used by itself or with something else?'   'Is it used in a house?'   'In which room of the house?'

'Is it used for cooking?'   'Why is it decorated?'

Learning story three

Turning the ideas in M is for mysterious objects around, I wanted the children to take a fresh look at their surroundings; to see if the commonplace could be mysterious.

I worked with a class of 30 vertically grouped seven, eight, and nine year old children at an inner city school, in various groupings over several lessons to encompass English, drama, geography, science, and art. This was a half term project, equivalent to two full afternoons a week.

A dying planet

In a whole class discussion, the children imagined that our home planet was dying, since one of our suns was moving closer to us. This gave us reason to explore the universe and eventually land on earth, to find a new home.

We all became aliens through role play, enabled by costume, face paint, and invented names. This activity was a way in to learning about space (science), and when we eventually landed, our local environment (geography). It also incorporated English, drama and art, in context. It included photography and photographic processes that don't require a darkroom (art) as well as using tape recorders to record interviews with members of the public (English). All of this culminated in a whole class diary/journal which recorded what they were interested in.

There were some initial sessions to develop the children's ideas about the home planet's plight, to create their characters in role, and to sustain them. I had already primed local shopkeepers, and the community beat officer (CBO). The CBO's imagination was fired up by the project to the extent that he produced a certificate giving the children permission to park their landing craft on the playground, which lent authenticity to the project.

We took trips out of school

On one of the visits children took photographs of objects they found mysterious on their walk. They looked at these back at school and reflected on what they had chosen to capture, and why they had made their choices. Images included: small animals, like dogs and cats; the red pillar-box; corners of brick walls; bicycle seats, entire bicycles and cyclists.

They were intrigued by the animals and wondered what it was that determined which end was the front and which the back. Of a small terrier, some children asked:
'Which end is its front?'
'Why is it on a string?'
'Will it run away?'
'What is it for?'

The interest in the corners of brick wall was a surprise for me – they were fixated on the pattern and how corners worked – what happened to the bricks to make them turn a corner? They focused on its construction and asked:
'Why does it make that pattern?'
'Is that half a brick?'
'How do you get half-bricks?'
'Is it just a whole brick the other way around?'

The red-painted cylindrical pillar-box with its large slot for letters was deemed to be potentially some kind of thing that could devour them, if they got too close. They asked:
'Why is it a cylinder?'
'Is it dangerous?'
'It could try to eat me – look at that mouth!'

The bicycle saddle was another surprise, with observations and questions which included:
'It's a triangle.'
'It's smooth.'
'Could it be comfortable?'

Visits as aliens

On another occasion children visited a local art gallery as aliens. This was interesting from the point of view of how they perceived framed works of art, while standing in another's shoes. One child commented that:
'It's like we are looking through a window right into the picture.'

They had experienced the opportunity to look at the everyday from a different angle, to perceive shapes, textures, and juxtapositions of things they would normally pass by without looking, or comment.

They were given time to conceive of the everyday in a new way – to view objects from a totally disinterested point of view and to speculate as to function, purpose and aesthetic qualities.

They were given time to walk in a different person's shoes, AND to see themselves and their environment from another point of view.

Their questions and queries were an eye-opener for me, as I could not have predicted the objects they would find mysterious, nor their responses to the commonplace.

Even if you plan everything with reference to the National Curriculum, it is still possible to follow an expanding idea across several subjects, but you have to be flexible and confident.

Role play enabled less confident children to ask questions they might otherwise be too diffident to ask.

What will I do next?

Next time I would narrow the approach to the photographic element, and see if using a camera alone can make children look at things differently.

I would also try using other viewfinders, such as home made card windows and magnifiers to look through to view the world, and ask them to bring in objects of their own that they find mysterious and worthy of speculation.

I would spend more time on possible routes of enquiry for their questions, because we never really did think about what dogs are for, or try out different bicycle saddles, or even think about the need for cylindrical letter boxes.

Learning story four

The dustbin game

A weekend's worth of clean rubbish was collected from a household and distributed amongst the children. The children were invited to make deductions about the household from the rubbish.

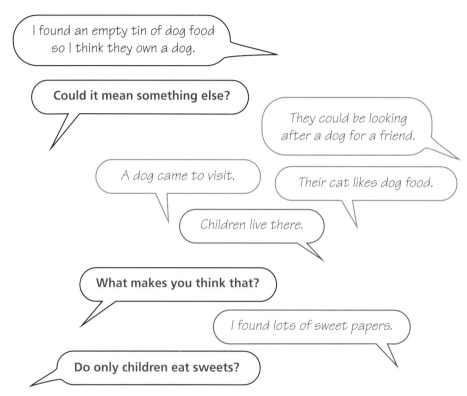

A five year old child came to a strongly held conviction when the children discovered empty water bottles in the rubbish. He was convinced the household had 'bad water'. Several months prior to this activity the local water supply was contaminated and all households were given bottled water and told not to use the mains supply.

This is a good example of how children store up past experiences for future reference, and draw on them to make sense of new experience.

N is for nothing

WHAT MATTERS TO CHILDREN
What's in the world? What isn't in the world? Who or what doesn't belong in the world – and why? What's gone missing? Why?

QUESTIONS WORTH ASKING
Where is nowhere? What is nothing? Is there a book that nobody wrote? Who is nobody? Can you hear nothing? Can you make nothing? Can you weigh nothing? Can YOU weigh nothing? Is air nothing? How big is nothing? How small is nothing? What isn't in the world? (fairness/peace/water/freedom…) When do you get to the end of never? Why is space called space? Where do people go to when they're not there?

In preventing play we tread a perilous path toward an uncertain future.
Sally Jenkinson

TOOLS
cloak of invisibility
Gollum's ring
rubbers
vacuum cleaners
vacuum flasks
off switches
delete buttons
invisible ink (lemon juice and fluids)
'no' signs – no smoking, no fishing, no mobile phones, no dogs, no entry…
magic slates

COLLECT
things that weigh nothing or next to nothing
words about nothing
  extinct
  nowt
  never
  no
  no-one
  cease
  desist…
air
the emptiest thing
x-rays

BIG IDEAS
never
absence
permanence
silence
inclusion
exclusion
space
loss
loneliness
abandonment

MAKE
filling and emptying
finding the emptiest thing
listening to nothing
making nothing
looking at nothing
feeling nothing
packing and unpacking suitcases
filling and emptying with…sand, gravel, mud, water
explore empty places, deserted places
empty plates, jugs, bowls, ovens
mime

BOOKS
Dogger — Shirley Hughes
Grandpa — John Burningham
Magpie Song — Laurence Anholt
Nothing — Mick Inkpen

POEMS
Nix, Nought, Nothing — J. Jacobs
No! — Thomas Hood

THINK AND TALK ABOUT NO!
Does no always mean no?
When do you say no? To whom? Why?
How does saying no make you feel?
How does being said 'no' to make you feel?

INVESTIGATE
empty number lines
0=zero
counting backwards
minus numbers
Edward Hopper paintings
being with nobody
Where can you find nothing?
Where can you find silence?
Stories, poems, music and artworks by Anon

MUSIC
Silent Music John Cage
Nowhere Man The Beatles
Sound of Silence Simon and Garfunkel
Silences (short and long)
How quietly can you play so no one can hear?

NOBODY
nobody to play with me nobody loves me nobody lives there anymore nobody listens to me nobody told me nobody lets me nobody chooses me nobody asks me

O is for **opposites**

WHAT MATTERS TO CHILDREN making sense of the world; being in the world; how the world works

DISCUSS

**birth and death
of people/
animals/plants**

**life cycles –
frog spawn
to frog,
egg to butterfly,
seed to fruit**

BOOKS

Big Little Leslie Petricelli
Change Anthony Browne
Dinosaurs Roar! Paul and Henrietta Stickland
Follow my Leader Emma Chichester Clarke
Growing Frogs Vivian French
Quiet Loud Leslie Petricelli
The Ugly Duckling Hans Christian Andersen

BIG IDEAS

classifying, comparing, variety, singularity

COLLECT

real things that are real opposites
real things that are almost opposites
things that are opposites that you can feel, see,
hear, taste and smell
words that are opposites

sweet/sour	hot/cold	straight/wavy
open/close	dull/shiny	long/short
prickly/smooth	flexible/firm	wet/dry
ugly/beautiful	high/low	day/night
plus/minus	live/dead	hill/valley
loud/quiet	hard/soft	

Can you collect real things to match the words?
sounds which are loud and quiet – door
slamming, buzzing insect…

INVESTIGATE

different ways you can make something or
yourself go

in/out	up/down	under/over
through/around	on/off…	

constructions - building high and low
things which can be pushed and pulled (train
set, wheelbarrow, swing, a friend, model
vehicles…)
things which open and close (eyes, books, hands,
doors, windows, jars, boxes…)
things which you can make

stop and go   large and small
fast and slow…

straight and wavy
with mark making tools
by modelling with clay, paper, dough,
by creating different hair styles…

ways of turning words into opposites with
pictures or collections of real objects or acting
them out

able/unable	kind/unkind
stick/unstick	inflate/deflate
true/untrue	edible/inedible
zip/unzip	respect/disrespect
similar/dissimilar	

stories with opposites
light and dark places with torches

MAKE

dry things wet and wet things dry
music with high and low sounds, with quiet
and loud episodes…
paintings with light and dark colours,
about day and night…
hot and cold food for a picnic or party
short and long zig-zag books
a play or dance of opposites
a picture of a mirror image of a mirror
image
paint or draw your own mirror image
work opposite a partner and be their
mirror image
turn a light place into somewhere dark
use the hand you do not usually use
design/make clothes for hot and cold
weather

QUESTIONS WORTH ASKING

What is the opposite of rabbit, umbrella, tree, sock?
Is there an opposite of opposite?
What makes an opposite opposite?
Is toast the opposite of bread?
Are there opposites of every feeling you have?
What things have no opposites?
Can you have a good and bad idea at the same time? What makes them so?
What does sitting opposite someone mean?
Is your reflection your opposite?
Why is the world upside down in a puddle?
Do numbers and shapes have opposites?
Has everything got an opposite?
What is the opposite of everybody?

*Most people think of success and
failure as opposites, but they both
are products of the same process.*

Roger von Oech

O is for opposites

Most people think of success and failure as opposites, but they both are products of the same process.

Roger von Oech

BIG IDEAS
classifying, comparing, variety, singularity

QUESTIONS WORTH ASKING
What is the opposite of 'rabbit', 'umbrella', 'tree', 'sock'?
Is there an opposite of opposites?
What makes an opposite opposite?
Is toast the opposite of bread?
Are there opposites of every feeling you have?
What things have no opposites?
Can you have a good and bad idea at the same time? What makes them so?
What does sitting opposite someone means?
Is your reflection your opposite?
Why is the world upside down in a puddle?
Do numbers and shapes have opposites?
Has everything got an opposite?
What is the opposite of everybody?

INVESTIGATE
different ways you can make something or
yourself go
in/out   up/down   under/over
through/around   on/off...
low and high
constructions - building high and low
things which can be pushed and pulled (train
set, wheelbarrow, swing, a friend), model
things which open and close (eyes, books, hands,
vehicles...)
things which you can make
doors, windows, lids, boxes...)
fast and slow...
stop and go   large and small
straight and way
tools making work
with walk making tool
by modelling with clay, paper, dough,
by creating different light styles...
ways of turning words into opposites with
picture or collections of real objects or acting
them out

hide/unhide   kind/unkind
stick/unstick   inflatable/deflatable
true/untrue   edible/inedible
zip/unzip   respect/disrespect
similar/dissimilar

stories with opposites
light and dark places with torches

COLLECT
real things that are real opposite
real things that are almost opposite
things that are opposites that you can feel, see,
heat, taste and smell
words that are opposites

sweet/sour   hot/cold
open/close   dull/shiny
prickly/smooth   flexible/firm
high/low   night/day
plus/minus   living/dead
long/quiet   hard/soft

Can you collect real things to match the words?
sounds which are loud and quiet – loop
jamming, buzzing insect...

MAKE
any things wet and any things dry
music with high and low sounds, music with quiet
and loud sounds...
painting with light and dark colours,
bright and day...
about day and night...
hot food and cold food for a picnic or party
about big-size books
should dance or play of opposites
a picture of a mirror image of a mirror
image
paint or draw your own mirror inside
work opposites a partner and their
mirror image
turn a light place into somewhere dark
use the hand you do not usually use
design/make clothes for hot and cold
weather

BOOKS
Big Little   Leslie Patricelli!!
Change   Anthony Browne
Dinosaur Roar   Paul and Henrietta Stickland
Follow my Leader   Emma Chichester Clarke
Growing Frogs   Vivian French
Quiet Loud   Leslie Patricelli!!
The Ugly Duckling   Hans Christian Andersen

DISCUSS
birth and death
groups of people/
study/examine...
life cycles – from
from spawn to frog,
to frog, to
egg to butterfly
seed to fruit

P is for *physical*

WHAT MATTERS TO CHILDREN   making sense of the world; moving around in the world

LOOK AT

the way birds walk – especially the head of a pigeon and the tail of a wagtail

the pathways of swifts

the way cats: walk, sit, wash, stretch, pounce

yourself in a full length mirror and show you are: sad, happy, angry, sleepy

The artworks:

Boccioni *Dynamism of a Soccer Player* and *Unique Forms of Continuity in Space*

Balla *Dynamism of a Dog on a Leash* and *Girl Running on a Balcony*

Degas *Dancer Drawings*

Gormley *RhIZome 1, 11 and 111* sculptures

QUESTIONS WORTH ASKING

Can the grass dance?
Can water dance?
Can clouds dance?
Can paint dance?

Do the stars dance in Van Gogh's *Starry Night*?

Does the sky dance in Turner's *Rain Steam and Speed*?

BOOKS

Bumpus Jumpus Dinosaurumpus Tony Mitton

Cloud Dance   Thomas Locker

Dinosaur Stomp! A Monster Pop-up Book
                             Paul Stickland

Down by the Cool of the Pool   Tony Mitton

Giraffes Can't Dance   Giles Andreae

Sailor Boy Jig   Margaret Wise Brown

VISIT

dance theatres or host a dance theatre company

zoos, wildlife and municipal parks to observe animal motion

swimming pools

big spaces

I always loved running...it was something you could do by yourself, and under your own power. You could go in any direction, fast or slow as you wanted, fighting the wind if you felt like it, seeking out new sights just on the strength of your feet and the courage of your lungs.
Jesse Owens

MAKE

a dance about...

a pigeon and a wagtail

upper body dances while sitting

lower body dances while sitting

whole body dances – a dinosaurumpus

MUSIC

Which untuned percussion instruments sound like: fish gliding, bird flapping, cat stretching, feet on the playground? make a playground symphony

DRAW/PAINT

lines that:

race; bounce; roll; hop; skip; loop; dawdle; zig-zag

look at Australian Aboriginal paintings of, for example, hunting and marks made to represent human or animal tracks

make oil pastel pathways

BIG IDEAS

friction
resistance
rhythm
energy and fuel

INVESTIGATE

rolling down a slope – and up again

how fast you can run in deep sand

how fast you can run in knee-deep water

how fast you can clap under water

how still you can be

the fastest/slowest/furthest/highest/lowest you can do anything

how long you can run before you run out of steam – and what it means

how unipeds, bipeds, quadrupeds and multipeds move

P is for physical
A learning story

Our school is a small Church of England primary in a village just outside a city. In the second half of the autumn term in the lead up to Christmas, we told the story of the Little Fir Tree to the vertically grouped class of 27 five to eight year olds, and we listened to the accompanying music, which is available on CD. It was hoped that, if the children found the idea inspiring, we could incorporate dance, music and drama into the whole experience, culminating in a performance for the school and the parents. We have fir trees in the school grounds, and took the children to look at them. The children brought in boughs of fir to handle and smell.

They found the story very appealing; they liked the music, with its variety of rhythms, and were attracted by the songs that they were going to learn. Five aspects of the story of the small tree out in the woods with the wild animals and the elements seemed to call for dance: the children playing in the woods, the rain, the sun, the snow, and the animals. Snow was not something that we could provide as a first hand experience, but we had photographs from last year's snowfall. They enjoyed looking out of the window at the rain and sun and going outside to explore them.

The entire project took place over approximately six hour long sessions. To begin with, snippets of the music were played to the children that illustrated the elements we proposed to use for dance. After a warm up and retelling the story a section at a time, the children improvised and explored appropriate movements and actions for rain, sun, snow and animals.

As the improvisation and explorations were under way, suggestions for variety were offered which encompassed such ideas as changes of level, speed and direction, building on their work in reception and year one. The children tried out their ideas; time was allowed to practise and be reflective, which helped them make their actions more interesting. The actions were generally travelling in different ways on the feet (creeping, tiptoeing, ambling, trotting, gliding, floating) to suggest the animals of the forest, using a variety of tempi and pathways; and for rain and snow, actions both on the spot and travelling, which also included arm and hand movements.

The children were asked to choose from all of the actions we had improvised, and having explored a range, to put their own selection of movements together. They watched each other's work and discussed which movements represented each element best. They suggested improvements. The aim was for children to agree on which actions from the range best suited the themes rain, sun, snow and animals. Gradually, the children decided on the sequences they would select for the final piece, and we worked together on refining them.

Some children chose to take the part of the fir trees, who were essentially static, some chose to take the part of children and animals, others chose to take the part of suns, rain, and snow. The six to seven year old children chose the parts of the animals and children, and developed their dances into more structured sequences that were repeated. The five to six year old children developed different sections to their dance and changed positions to correspond to the changes in the music.

Since they had essentially composed their sequences themselves, they memorised them quickly, and we tried the sequences with the songs intermingled. The rhythmic music gave them further inspiration to perform, and once costumes were provided, they began to conceive of the performance as a large finished whole, of which their dances were a necessary, integral, and exciting part.

The children were very reflective about their work, and were really exciting to work with, as they developed their dances in ways that had not been anticipated. The eight to ten year old vertically grouped class watched the dances, and wrote appreciative reviews for their 'recount' work in literacy. This made the children really proud of their work. They watched a video of their performance at the end, and later it was wonderful to see everyone acting out each other's dances with great enthusiasm.

Children reflect on their dance

The children playing

It was good music for running and bouncing and playing hide and seek.

It sounded as though the music was running everywhere.

It was exciting when it started.

It was fun learning the patterns and weaving in and out of the trees.

Sun

The movement was slower and more gentle.

I liked moving my hands like the rays of the sun.

I felt hot because the sun looked hot.

I liked being on the block and turning round.

I liked moving in a pattern and holding hands.

Snow

This was a group of very active boys who really focused on their work, operating at high levels of concentration and interpretation.

They maybe felt really cold.

I liked turning round and round and felt like a real snowflake falling.

I liked moving in a pattern and holding hands.

I liked going up and down.

I liked the way they landed round the little fir tree at the end.

Rain

I liked the arm movements.

Jack had the different rhythms and used lots of different levels.

I felt like a raindrop.

Rain is wet!

Animals

It made me feel happy and I liked dancing round the tree.

It was important that I kept in the space close to the tree because I had to go and cheer the little fir tree up first, so needed to be ready.

We had to remember our sequences and do it together

I raised my arms up on the beat after everyone else and that looked really good.

I liked the little fir tree skipping in the middle of the animals in the last part when they had cheered her up.

Q is for questions

The educator's responsibility for children's questions – what needs doing?

Value every question as a genuine enquiry.

Listen to children's questions and write them down (see following page).

Respect children's questions – see them as a search for meaning in the world.

Make sure that all children have equal opportunities to ask questions.

Respond to children's questions in a variety of ways:

- *with first hand experiences (activities, visits, visitors) to take their learning on*
- *with discussion and debate, sharing their questions with others (children and adults)*
- *by helping them to make connections with other areas of their experiences*
- *by using relevant story books.*

Don't assume that it is the teacher's job to ask the questions and the children's task to answer them.

Remember, the more questions adults ask children, the less time there is for discussing children's questions, or for children to ask any.

Introduction: questions worth asking and children's questions

Throughout the writing of this book we have been worrying about the balance between trying to be helpful to educators, and doing too much of their thinking for them. Too many helpful suggestions can be just as hard to handle as too few. The issue of questions is a particularly tricky one in this respect. We know from dozens of classroom studies that teachers ask an extraordinary number of questions: we don't need to encourage them to ask more. But we also know that many of these questions are the wrong kind to stimulate children's thinking or support their learning. Many questions simply ask children to remember rather than explain, connect, pull it all together, imagine, invent new possibilities, compare, contrast, argue, reason…all the kinds of thinking we want children to do as they explore the world around them.

We have tried to solve this problem by including, on every page, a section called QUESTIONS WORTH ASKING. These are questions we hope will open up possibilities for exploring the topics we have selected: they are not the only questions that could be asked, but we hope they demonstrate how an unexpected question can lead to unexpected insights, unpredictable discoveries, and rich, meaningful learning. Questions stimulate quests to unknown territories and to far horizons. But by solving the problem in this way, we may have created another. We may unintentionally have suggested that the questions adults ask are more important and worthwhile than the questions children ask. On the contrary, we think children's questions are especially important starting points for the kinds of projects and enquiries we are advocating in this book.

Hypothesis or question – what is the difference?

Some of the educators who participated in the development of this book commented that some children make statements or formulate hypotheses, rather than ask questions. For example, one educator quoted a child who said:
'Everybody is symmetrical except dead people.'

This is, grammatically speaking, a statement. But how simple (and how exciting) to take this statement, and reframe it as a question for other children to debate and discuss. Not just 'What do you think of Susan's idea?' but, 'Are people symmetrical? All people? Tall and short? Old and young? Living and dead?' and so on. It's well worth listening to children's talk for interesting and provocative ideas that could be turned into questions for worthwhile discussions.

CHILDREN'S QUESTIONS

We have long been fascinated by children's questions and the evidence they constitute of children's capacity for complex and innovative thinking. From our collections of children's questions, we have selected some examples that we hope will convince our readers that listening to children's questions is always a rewarding and worthwhile activity. The examples fall into two categories.

1

THEIR QUESTIONS ABOUT RULES, ROUTINES AND PROCEDURES

Is mine better?
Can I go now?
Does it matter who wins?
Where shall I start?
Please can I turn over?
Do I have to?
Who's going to look after us?
Can it be tomorrow?
If I wear tights, am I still a boy?

COMMENT

These questions illustrate children's concern both with doing things right and getting things right (related but not synonymous categories). The children also seem to be concerned with what lies behind the procedures, perhaps even expressing an anxiety that there isn't very much in the way of rhyme or reason behind the rules and regulations by which they are required to abide. One interpretation of these questions is that they are the questions of children who are learning to be dependent and obedient, at the expense of learning to be exploratory, adventurous free thinkers. As such they are useful feedback to practitioners who can learn, from questions like these, the extent to which their classroom rules make any kind of human sense to the children. But there are other, more rewarding questions that children ask.

2

THEIR QUESTIONS ABOUT THE WORLD OUTSIDE THE CLASSROOM

Why is the moon broken today?
Why do fireworks go up?
Why don't plants grow in the moonlight?
Why can you see through glass when it's made of sand?
Would a polar bear melt in the desert?
What is love?
Can children make a bed?
Do cats have to chase mice in real life?
Why are you pretty? Why aren't you pretty?
When I ask a question, where does it come from?

COMMENT

These questions are, we believe, very different. They show children reaching out beyond the four walls of their setting into distant domains. In formal terms we can see the worlds of astronomy, physics, biology, psychology, philosophy and the huge world of emotional experience in which these children are already seasoned travellers. These children are exploratory, adventurous and free-thinking. They are learning about a wider and more intriguing world than the enclosed space of their benign classrooms. They are enthused by the world's mysteries and its contrasts. Any of these questions is not just worth asking, it is worth taking seriously, exploring it and, of course, learning from it.

Q is for questions

Annabelle Dixon worked as an educator of children for many years and always kept a question book. She says:

How did I keep a question book?

I used to wear an apron with lots of pockets. People teased me about it, but I needed pockets for my little notebooks. I recorded children's questions as part of my daily routine. I just wrote them down. I didn't bother with functional questions like 'Where do the pencils go?' or 'Are we going to assembly?' although of course, these may have told me something about particular children. I wrote down the children's questions that involved: finding out, solving problems, reaching a conclusion or asking more questions. In the book area I kept a large 'Book of Questions' where I wrote down those the children asked to be recorded; it was often used at discussion times. I also noted down their comments about all the things they found out. I did it all the time, wherever we were.

If children are doing something worthwhile they will never waste time. They might act on it in ways you don't expect, but they don't waste time.

Annabelle Dixon

Why did I keep a question book?

I first did this because of the influence that Piaget and Susan and Nathan Isaacs had on my work with children. I wanted to push the edges of their learning on as far as I could. In order to do this I needed to know what it was they wanted to learn. The questions they were asking became one of my tools for finding this out. Above all it helped me find out their level of thinking, which is very easy to mistake with young children; they really do think differently. I couldn't work without them as a guide, aid to reflection and source of feedback.

Examples from the question book

'Can I put the baby toads in with the baby frogs to compare them?'

'When does the future start?'

(Child watching and feeling water trickle through her hands as she plays in a water tray) 'Why doesn't water have bones?'

'When did people first think of language?'

'I've found out that when this bottle's empty it floats, but when it's full it sinks. Why does it do that?'

'How come little girls don't always do what their mummies ask?'

What did I do with the questions?

Some questions were answered then and there, but others needed more of an exploration. I always asked children if they wanted their question to be shared with others. During the day I would feed back the ones I had permission to share. Children would offer suggestions and ideas. Some would team up to try and solve a problem and take the investigation further. Some preferred to work alone but they grew to value team work.

The children's questions led the curriculum. As a professional, I knew the learning potential each one offered and I monitored what was done, and all the children's achievements.

The children's questions determined what resources they might need and what activities, visits and materials could best support them. The children had ideas for activities too, which I included in my planning.

The gradual introduction of tool words meant that these became part of the resources that were used for exploration. (See also tool words below.)

Keeping a question book

What was the effect on the children?

Children knew that their questions were taken seriously but not always answered immediately. They came to recognise that there were ways they could answer their own questions and/or that they could share them with others. The classroom culture was such that 'not knowing' and wanting to 'find out' were not only acceptable but could offer new excitements and insights. 'What if' and 'why' led them to view new experiences (or revisit old ones) at a level of real engagement, both emotional and intellectual. The 'tool words' became part of their everyday vocabulary, and were used at home as well as at school.

It was rewarding when children began to find things out for themselves and recognised their own and each other's achievements.

Annabelle Dixon

Practical suggestions for educators

There must be things for children to ask questions about. If there aren't any things there won't be any questions!

Avoid creating an all plastic environment. The hidden sterility gets passed on.

Have plenty of natural materials and objects for children to investigate – some identifiable and some not immediately so.

Let children look, touch and explore for as long as they want to, in ways they choose for themselves.

Regularly change resources.

Stand back and let children explore, test things out, find things out and make meanings.

Help children develop the tools they need for asking questions by introducing language for exploring both things and ideas. (See also tool words.)

Introducing 'tool words' helped children ask questions and find things out. Some of the most important of these were:

identical
similar
different
organise
comment
question
agree
disagree
problem
team work
respect
think
imagination
mystery
decision
challenge
compare
series
set
opposite
pattern
solution
detail
'I've found out…'

Children need lots of experience in using these words, which are introduced gradually and in context. Under these conditions children discover what they really mean and use them effectively.

Questions about questions

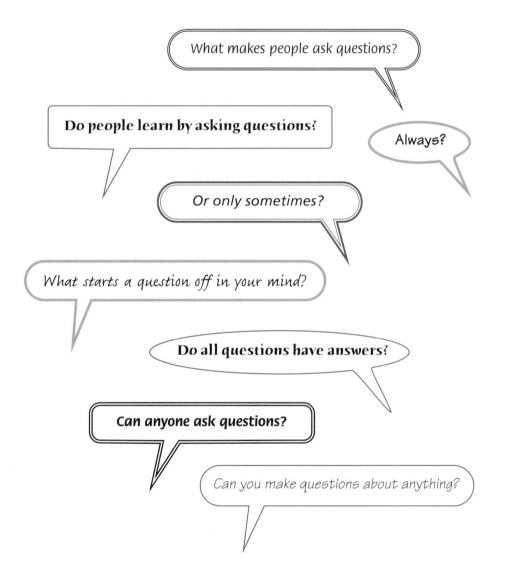

What makes people ask questions?

Do people learn by asking questions?

Always?

Or only sometimes?

What starts a question off in your mind?

Do all questions have answers?

Can anyone ask questions?

Can you make questions about anything?

What kinds of questions do people ask?

What kinds of questions do grown ups ask?

What kinds of questions do children ask?

What kinds of questions do mothers ask?

What kinds of questions do fathers ask?

What kinds of questions do babies ask?

What kinds of questions do doctors ask?

What kinds of questions do teachers ask?

What kinds of questions do gardeners ask?

What kinds of questions do astronauts ask?

What kinds of questions do sailors ask?

What kinds of questions do asylum seekers ask?

What kinds of questions do dancers ask?

What kinds of questions do princes and princesses ask?

What kinds of questions do imams, rabbis and vicars ask?

What kinds of questions do prisoners ask?

What kinds of questions do government ministers ask?

What kinds of questions do mermaids ask?

What kinds of questions do geologists, oceanographers and botanists ask?

What would happen if people weren't allowed to ask questions? Can a poem be a question? Can you answer a question with a question?

Children's difficult questions

Children sometimes ask us questions that may seem personal, cheeky, philosophical, embarrassing, revealing, quirky or prejudiced – and certainly difficult to answer.

Children expect the help and truthfulness of grown-ups.

Loris Malaguzzi

Educators need to be confident enough to be honest with children. This entails:

  being well informed about relevant political and cultural issues, both local and worldwide

  working as a staff group, anticipating questions and formulating sensitive responses

  critically examining personal values

  being clear about the values shared and agreed by the whole staff group.

Being helpful and truthful means:

  listening to these questions attentively, without making assumptions or judgements and without blaming or scolding the children

  sometimes saying that you don't know, but are prepared to find out or give it more thought

  supporting and encouraging children in thinking through the effect of their words and actions on others, seeing how words can hurt, and how the 'kindness of children' can prevail.

Some further suggestions for responding to children's difficult questions are given in *Action for Racial Equality in the Early Years: Understanding the Past, Thinking about the Present, Planning for the Future* by Jane Lane.

Why aren't you pretty?

Why doesn't praying work?

Why does Vasos keep making that noise?

Why does she smell funny?

Why did Fiona's brother get blown up?

Is she made of chocolate?

Are soldiers good or bad?

Why can't I call him 'Paki' when everyone else does?

Why is Johnny going to die next year?

Why has Sarah got two mummies?

 R is for rain

WHAT MATTERS TO CHILDREN things the world is made of; how the world works; being in the world

VISITS
visit the rain at many different places
pumping station
reservoir
drains
fountains
gargoyles

EXPERIMENT WITH
hoses
funnels
guttering
pepper pot/flour sifter
sieves
buckets
watering can
sprinkler
turkey baster
wheelbarrows
water hoover
mops
sponges
big broom
water butt
water pump
water wheel
absorbent materials
water repellent materials
hairdryers
umbrellas
wellies

BIG IDEAS
solubility, absorbent and repellent material, protection, evaporation water – one of the four elements

BOOKS
Alfie's Feet — Shirley Hughes
The Hundred Languages of Children
Exhibition Catalogue — Reggio Children
Guinness Book of Records
James and the Rain — Reg Cartwright
Rain — Manya Stojic
Rainy Day — Emma Haughton

All children have the right to enjoy the essential and special nature of being outdoors.   Learning Through Landscapes

QUESTIONS WORTH ASKING
When is a cloud a rain cloud? How big is the biggest puddle? Is a reservoir a puddle? When is a puddle a pond? When is a puddle a flood? Why does rain come down? Does rain always go down? What makes rain bounce? Does all rain bounce? Is all mud rain mud? When does rain stop being rain? Why does rain go sideways? Does it rain on Mars? Is all rain the same? Is there any water that is not rain? Can you make a rain forest? Where does the rain go (in the place you live/at your school/at the park/at a cathedral)? Is dog spit rain? Who likes rain? What happens when there is no rain?

MAKE
rain
bird baths
rain go down gutters
things and surfaces to keep rain off
make puddles (in mud, tarmac, shingle, sand)
make rain go away
make puddles and water disappear
rain paint
rain mud
a rain dance
rain music

COLLECT
pictures of the rain by
  Hokusai
  Hiroshige
  Renoir
  Rousseau
words about rain
  drizzle
  mist
  monsoon
  soak
  steep
  sea fret
  gushing
  pouring
  splash
  cats and dogs
  drench
rain clothes
umbrellas

MUSIC
I Can't Stand the Rain, Pitter Patter Raindrops, use rain sticks, make your own rain sounds, Rain Drops Keep Falling on my Head, Rain Drop Prelude, Raining in my Heart, Singing in the Rain (and the video of the dance too), Why Does it Always Rain on Me?

INVESTIGATE
- **different ways of collecting rain**
- **how to change rain water – freeze and heat**
- **adding substances to rain water – sand, food colouring, corn flour**
- **where rain can be found**
- **objects which float on rain**
- **protection from rain – homes, clothing**
- **what rain feels, sounds and smells like**
- **what happens when there is too much rain (flooding) too little rain, and no rain (drought)**
- **animals in the rain**
- **worms coming out when it's raining**
- **how the world looks before it's rained**
- **how the world looks when it's rained**
- **how the world looks after it's rained**
- **how the world smells after it's rained**
- **rain clouds**
- **puddle depths, shapes and sizes**
- **the colour of rain**
- **visit an umbrella shop**

R is for rain

A learning story

In a one-class entry infants school in a large industrial city, the teachers and children worked together to install an exhibition of UMBRELLAS in the school hall, to entertain parents and families on the termly open evening. Every imaginable kind of umbrella was represented, from tiny cocktail stick umbrellas to a huge dark green angler's umbrella. The school photographer was persuaded to lend her silver umbrella; there were umbrella skeletons, parasols, bamboo umbrellas and many, many more. Children's observational drawings and clay models were added to the exhibition, together with documentation of the work of small discussion groups investigating the topic of umbrellas through talk. The contributions given below come from one such group, in a mixed class of five, six and seven year olds.

'They go up and down.'
'Children's ones are smaller.'
'They keep you dry – not all of you.'
'You'd have to have a very big one to keep your feet dry.'
'Babies have an umbrella on their pram – for the sun.'
'Golf people have umbrellas.'
'Without an umbrella your hair gets wet.'
'Sometimes tables have umbrellas.'
'Parasols are umbrellas.'
'Umbrellas are made of plastic, cloth, metal, wood.'
'People use them in the wet, not in the dry – except on the beach.'
'Umbrellas have to have handles.'
'An elephant doesn't use an umbrella – it's too big.'
'Fishes don't use umbrellas.'
'The umbrella for a monkey is a tree.'
'A bus shelter is like an umbrella.'

'Umbrella pines are a kind of tree.'
'You can use an umbrella when you open a champagne bottle.'
'Don't use one in the shower – you won't get clean.'
'The roof is an umbrella to the house.'
'The shell is an umbrella to the tortoise.'
'Robots need them for the rust.'
'A mushroom is an umbrella to a mouse.'
'A rainbow is shaped like an umbrella.'
'A hat or a jumper, or a newspaper, or a hood – all good umbrellas.'
'The fleece is an umbrella for the sheep.'
'A flower is an umbrella for the bee.'
'A helmet is like an umbrella.'
'Goggles are umbrellas for your eyes.'
'A greenhouse is an umbrella for plants.'
'Channel swimmers are covered in butter.'

(with acknowledgements to Alan, Alex, Bryony, Helen, Hendrix, Katherine and Sarah)

S is for surfaces

WHAT MATTERS TO CHILDREN   knowing the world; being in the world; making a mark on the world

INVESTIGATE

wet sand

dry sand

gravel

stones

bark

moss

clay

paper

textiles

shingle

INVESTIGATE

ways to add surfaces to things – icing a cake, tarmac, mulching a flower bed

wetting different surfaces

how many ways a surface can be changed

the textured pictures of the Boyle Family which represent the earth's surfaces

INVESTIGATE

how to make engravings, etchings, wood cuts, lino prints and other relief prints using polystyrene press print, string, card or textured papers

look at the engravings and woodcuts of Clifford Harper, Claire Leighton, Gwen Raverat, Thomas Bewick, Hiroshige, Hokusai

We are trying to make the best visual description our senses and our minds can achieve of a random sample of the reality that surrounds us. We want to see without motive and without reminiscence this cliff, this street, this roof, this field, this rock, this earth.
Mark Boyle

WORDS

prickly, smooth, floppy, silky, uneven, gritted, hairy, fluffy, crinkled, sharp, hard, gnarled, rutted, soft, squelchy, solid, jagged

MAKE

sand-casts	using wet sand and plaster of Paris
rubbings	of surfaces to use as a resource for a paper collage
collages	of textured papers or fabrics
clay	relief tiles
drawings	of objects hidden in 'feely bags' (draw by touch alone)
wool windings	to represent the texture and colour of natural objects such as shells, plants or stones
stitched surfaces	to represent the texture and colour of surfaces, such as woodland, desert, the sun
weavings	using a range of materials – threads, fabrics, plastic, grasses
paper landscapes	using twisted, pleated, pierced, embossed and rolled papers
paintings	using very thick paint or with additives such as glue, sand or sawdust
drawings	on different surfaces – papers, walls, the pavement, chalk boards, perspex, glass
a 'feely tunnel'	from cardboard boxes – line the interior surfaces with a range of materials to crawl through

BIG IDEAS
sensory awareness
transforming
representing
making

QUESTIONS WORTH ASKING
How deep is a surface? Have clouds got a surface? Is a surface the same as a skin? Where does the surface of skin start and stop? Where does the surface of a round ball start and finish?

BOOKS
Roosters Off to See the World	Eric Carle
Snail Trail	Ruth Brown
The Big Big Sea	Martin Waddell
The Wonderful World Book	Jennie Maizels and Kate Petty
We're Going on a Bear Hunt	Michael Rosen

S is for **surfaces**

A learning story

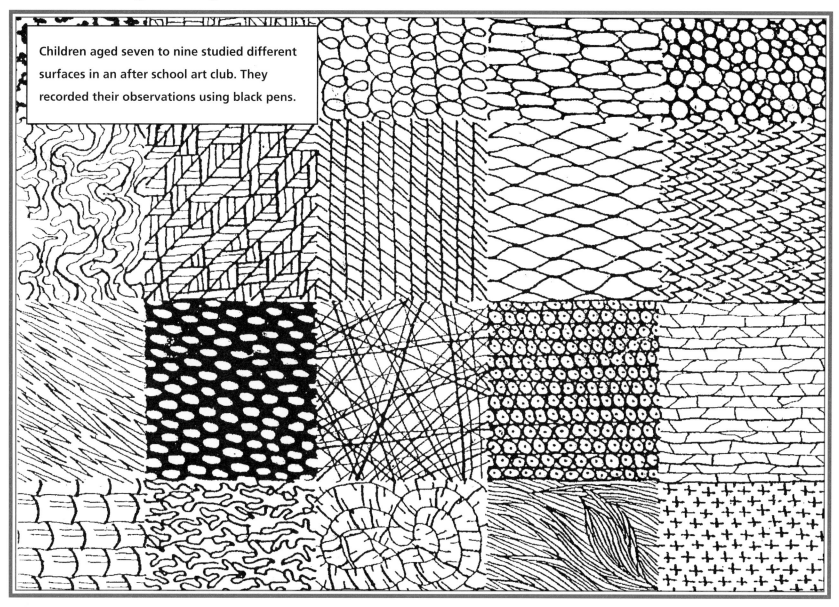

Children aged seven to nine studied different surfaces in an after school art club. They recorded their observations using black pens.

T is for Tate and other galleries

We have to nourish our feeling, and we can only do so with materials derived from the world around us. This is the process whereby the artist incorporates and gradually assimilates the external world within himself, until the object of his drawing has become like a part of his being.

Henri Matisse

BIG IDEAS
a language for life
a way of thinking and being
art is all around us

QUESTIONS WORTH ASKING
What is it made of? Is anything else made of the same material?
Why does it look like that?
How was it made?
Can I make one like it? What do I need?
What can you see?
What does it mean?
What do you think it is?
Do you like it? Why?

INVESTIGATE
- *different colours using paint and invent colour names, for example, banana yellow, speckled frog green…*
- *create a range of textures: smooth; spiky; stippled with paint; pencil, clay, wool…*
- *explore 3-D with paper, clay, card, boxes, dough, wet sand, wooden blocks…*
- *experiment with mark making using non-standard tools such as fingers, fists, backs of hands, toes, crumpled paper, stones, sticks…*

BOOKS
Animals in Art (Come Look with Me)	Gladys S. Blizzard
Degas and the Little Dancer	Laurence Anholt
I-Spy Transport in Art (and others in the series)	Lucy Micklethwait
Katie's Picture Show	James Mayhew
Oxford First Book of Art	Gillian Wolfe
Picasso and the Girl with the Ponytail	Laurence Anholt

MAKE
works of art –
paintings, drawings, carvings, prints, collages…

your own gallery and role play area

select work for an exhibition
- advertise – posters
- tickets
- private view and invitations
- café and refreshments
- gallery shop – sell your own reproductions
- security
- guides and guided tours

make a role play area based on a work of art (see the T is for Tate learning story)

VISIT
places with works of art – galleries, museums, shopping centres, sculpture parks, public buildings…

look at:
    paintings
    sculptures
    textiles – carpets, clothes, wall hangings
    pottery/ceramics
    photography
    furniture (see also F is for)
    costumes – armour
    books…

invite artists, crafts people or designers from a variety of cultures to talk to the children and to work alongside them

COLLECT
things you would like to keep for ever
your favourite works of art – made by yourself and/or made by others
colours and colour names (viridian, ultra marine…)
all things purple – aubergine, grapes, amethyst
art words:

portrait	batik	landscape	bas relief
triptych	mosaic	diptych	miniature
cameo	bust	torso	diorama
craquelure	pigment	dye	mendi
rangoli	tjanting		

patterns – natural and manufactured (fir cones, feathers, sunflower seed heads, cloth, roof tiles, drain covers…)

MUSIC
choose an instrument (for its sound) to represent the marks, shapes and colours in a painting, for example, claves for dots, triangle for zig-zags.

try using abstract painting initially – the works of Wassily Kandinsky, Jackson Pollock, Howard Hodgkin, Kalahari Bushmen…

explore making marks suggested by sounds heard – natural sounds or recorded

T is for Tate and other galleries
Learning stories

Learning story one

The Doctor by Sir Luke Fildes (1891)

This Victorian painting shows a doctor visiting a sick child. The cottage is gloomy and details are hard to see. There is no evidence of electricity or running water. A sickly child is lying under a blanket across two chairs with anxious parents looking on. On the floor of the cottage is an unrecognisable whitish 'something' positioned not far from the dangling arm of the ailing child. After studying the painting one child asked,

'What's that white thing?'

'I don't know. What do you think it could be?' asked the teacher. From there the flood gates opened. The children's thinking became as visible as the painting they were looking at. Some suggested it was a discarded tissue. Another ventured that a tissue was unlikely as they were not used in 'the olden days'. Perhaps it was a bandage? And so it went on. The ideas flowed. 'I think…' 'because…'

After the children had described the physical features of the picture they went on to speculate how the various people in the painting were feeling.

> I would never have believed my reception class could look at a picture so intently. One picture for half an hour!

> A good museum can offer so many first hand experiences to children. Often things we just can't replicate at school.

> Inviting an artist to work alongside the children in school had such an impact on their work.

> I would thoroughly recommend a visit to the National Gallery. The education officers are fantastic. It wasn't just the children who had a great time. We all left wanting more.

Learning story two

The Bedroom by Vincent Van Gogh (1889)

A class of six and seven year olds looked very carefully at the painting. They were so inspired by it that they constructed the painting in three dimensions in their role play area. The children were informed about Van Gogh's life and were told stories about him.

Everyone wanted to paint like Van Gogh and there was no shortage of volunteers who wanted to don the artist's straw hat and smock and paint outdoors. Van Gogh had a constant stream of visitors to his bedroom. The visitors requested paintings, trips out to the field to paint together, commissioned portraits, or just wanted to join in the art of convivial conversation. This was either around the popular wicker table and chairs complete with carafe and glasses or on the bed. Of course there were times when Van Gogh was too ill to summon enough energy to paint. The following conversation was overheard in the role play area:

(Child knocks on bedroom door) 'Vincent shall we go out to the field to paint?'

(Prostrate from beneath the red cover on the bed) 'No, not today. I'm feeling depressed.'

The Doctor can be viewed at www.tate.org.uk
The Bedroom can be viewed at www.vangoghgallery.com

T is for **thinking**

On these pages we summarise some of our own thoughts about children's thinking, the kinds of thinking that we value, the important kinds of thinking that are stimulated and fostered by the first hand experiences that we suggest on the other alphabet pages.

Taking thinking seriously

Everyone has a favourite story to tell of a child who comes out with an apparently absurd comment on the world and its inhabitants: we tend to treat these fantastic, bizarre, even surreal remarks as charming, or laughable, or cute. In this book, our argument is that all children's thinking, however surreal it may seem, deserves to be taken seriously, as rational reflections on their experiences, and as considered contributions to their growing understanding. Loris Malaguzzi argues forcibly that the logic of children's thought straddles two dimensions: the logic of imagination as well as the logic of things. These two domains co-exist in a relationship of both turbulence and reciprocity, a relationship in keeping with the natures and desires of children. Indeed, he goes on to claim, their very identity emerges through the process of 'bringing closer together the frontiers of the real world, those of the possible and the impossible'. Vivian Gussin Paley, a supreme practitioner of the art of taking children's thinking seriously, makes the same point in a different way. She observes how the children in her kindergarten often solve puzzles and problems in the real world by recourse to fantasy and fairy tale. For Paley, this is not a weakness, but a sign of admirable elasticity of thought. 'As soon as (a child) learns a language well enough, and before he is told he cannot invent the world, he will explain everything.' And, extending this thought, she explains:

> The five or six year old is...not a captive of his illusions and fantasies, but can choose them for support or stimulation...He has become aware of the thinking required by the adult world, but is not yet committed to its burden of rigid consistency.
>
> (Wally's Stories, p.81)

This is thinking well worth taking seriously.

THINKING WORDS
conceive
invent, find out
discover
imagine
contemplate, what if…
reason, wonder
sense
rationalise, predict
perhaps, maybe
believe
feel
consider
suppose
assume
puzzle, ponder
judge, mystery
pray
concentrate
thinking cap
reflect
study
wanderings
musing
foresight
afterthought
abstract
hindsight

We may seem inconsistent and unpredictable to you, but we think according to our own logic; we see the world from where we stand. We would like you to respect and value this, as our ways of seeing can tell you much about us. We are frequently offered watered-down material that is meant for older children, but we don't thrive on it. We think differently, and do best when this is recognized. Our ideas may seem bizarre, even anarchic at times, but that is because we haven't yet been conditioned into what is required of a 'pupil'. We are curious, spontaneous, enterprising and endlessly creative – when we're allowed to be. We are children, between three and eight: we are strong and powerful thinkers. Give us the opportunities to show it.

> *The headwork itself is most fruitful when it is also handwork and bodywork. In these [early] years, the child's intelligence is essentially practical. He thinks as much with his hands as with his tongue…*
>
> Susan Isaacs

> *From childhood we are on a special flight of wonder.*
>
> Albert Einstein

BOOKS FOR EDUCATORS

Intelligence Reframed: Multiple Intelligence for the 21st Century
Howard Gardner

Quality in Diversity
Early Childhood Forum

The Language and Thought of the Child
Jean Piaget

The Hundred Languages of Children – Advanced Reflections
editors Edwards. C, Gandini, L. and Forman G.

Thinking Children
Anne Meade with Pam Cubey

Threads of Thinking: Young Children Learning and the Role of Early Education
Cathy Nutbrown

Children thinking with their whole bodies

From an adult perspective it may be hard to acknowledge just how much we have been conditioned to take control of our bodies to mask our feelings. Some people may only let their feelings show at moments of extreme emotion, or when it is expected – throwing up their hands when a goal is scored, or happily applauding the school play.

Children's physical responses to the world are immediate and unmediated; as they touch, they discover, and confirm or puzzle and wonder. Often their responses are to the physicality they slowly realize they possess: witness the eight month old's unalloyed pleasure at bouncing, and jigging her arms up and down, in contrast to the sophistication of the eight year-old skipping, running, leapfrogging…

Gestures and actions gradually become ways of expressing thoughts, ideas and feelings; children don't have to puzzle out how to translate their feelings into physical action. They learn very quickly that certain actions embody and convey meaning to those around them: reaching up, stamping feet, shrugging, balling-up and shaking fists, kicking, hitting, headshaking, withdrawing, creeping, tiptoeing, and so forth, all of them culturally defined.

With sensitive support and encouragement, children's sensory and expressive repertoire deepens and becomes second nature; their thinking is made physically visible in just the same way as in their drawing or mark-making in paint. Their physicality gradually becomes a richer and more varied language of expression, which they can also perceive in the actions of others.

Through their whole bodies children learn about themselves and their environment. Through their own eyes, bones, joints, muscles, skin, heart and lungs, children experience directly the forces of the physical world: they learn to defy gravity by jumping so high they can fly; they learn how friction affects their speed on sand or in water; they learn about the expense of energy when they run until they drop; they learn about the centrifugal force of spinning and its dizzying effects.

Pioneering dancer and choreographer Martha Graham said:

This expression is unique. If you block it, it will never exist through any other medium and will be lost.

'Drawings don't just come from your hands, they come from your head too…because first you think and then you do the drawings with your hands.'

'It's fun to do the things you have in your mind. You do it with your hands and then the things you had in your head come out.'

'Ideas are in the brain, but they have to come out somewhere…. sometimes they come out of your mouth and sometimes they come out of your hand…hands have to think…'

(5 and 6 year old children from the Pablo Neruda School, Reggio Emilia

Making thinking visible

When children draw, paint, make a model, or a sculpture, or write a story or poem, their thinking becomes visible. We can see their response to experiences, real or imaginary. They show us what is important to them, what they have noticed and what they have felt. They use the tools and materials available to them to represent and express their thinking.

When children make their ideas visible in this way they think with the materials rather than before the materials are used. They plan as they make, adapting, changing, developing, enlarging, adding detail and definition to the work they are creating.

If we are to help children to express their thinking then the range and authenticity of the tools and materials are important, along with the knowledge of how they work. A range of mark making tools, collections of natural and made objects (feathers, shells, pebbles, buttons, cinnamon sticks, dried leaves, pipe cleaners and pompoms, fabric, threads, beads), card, clay, wire, wood, sand, mud and stone for working in 3-D make a rich palette of resources. They are irresistible: children will use them to explore, investigate, classify, arrange, design, solve problems, imagine, observe and translate. Each representation is personal and unique and the work of thoughtful hands.

Children thinking in their play

Children are expert thinkers. In play, they test out their ideas and theories; they recreate what they know of the world, from their own experiences. They work out 'what is' and 'what might be'. They experiment with materials and with other children to find out how things work and how things happen; they want to know how to make things happen for themselves. They test out what it is like to think inside many alternative worlds of reality and fantasy. They step into the shoes of others and think as they might think. They behave as others might behave. They take themselves on journeys into other worlds: a hospital, a hairdresser's, a veterinary surgery, Batman's cave, Hogwarts, a Traveller's trailer, or a mermaid lagoon. They check out rules of behaviour and social norms. They go on to invent and practise their own rules of behaviour and social norms.

Children play with the things of the world and the people of the world, in different places of the world. They explore the important themes of love and caring, good and bad, powerful and weak, loss and loneliness. They try to make sense of world events and current affairs. In their play they think about, 'Who am I?' Who might I become?' 'What will that be like?' 'How can I keep safe in my world?' They magnificently wonder, 'What if…?' In their play children make sense of the world.

Play is a form of thought.   Piaget

❝ I don't know whether you have ever seen a map of a person's mind. Doctors sometimes draw maps of other parts of you…but catch them trying to draw a map of a child's mind, which is not only confused, but keeps going round all the time. There are zig-zag lines on it, just like your temperature on a card, and these are probably roads in the island; for the Neverland is always more or less an island with astonishing splashes of colour here and there, and coral reefs and rakish-looking craft in the offing and savages and lonely lairs and gnomes who are mostly tailors, and a cave through which a river runs, and princes with six elder brothers, and a hut fast going to decay, and one very small old lady with a hooked nose. It would be an easy map if that were all: but there are also the first day at school, 'religion', fathers, the round pond, needlework, murders, hangings, verbs that take the dative, chocolate pudding day, getting into braces, say ninety-nine, three-pence for pulling out your tooth yourself and so on: and either these are part of the island or they are another map showing through, and it is all rather confusing, especially as nothing will stand still. ❞

J. M. Barrie, *Peter Pan and Wendy*

U is for **under**

WHAT MATTERS TO CHILDREN   things the world is made of; how the world works

MAKE

weavings – over one, under one, – over one, under three…
make a wormery or formicary
plant seeds – indoors and outdoors
play games involving under arm bowling
make an archaeological dig themed role play area
dance – oranges and lemons, in and out the dusky bluebells and other dances involving dancing under arches
stand under an umbrella, tin tray, plastic sheet… and listen to the rain
make tunnels, bridges, arches to walk, crawl, slide under
make camps, dens, caves and bridges…
bury treasure in the sandtray
bury treasure outside and go on a treasure hunt

It is, in fact, nothing short of a miracle that the modern methods of instruction have not yet entirely strangled the holy curiosity of inquiry; for this delicate little plant, aside from stimulation, stands mainly in need of freedom…
Albert Einstein

BIG IDEAS
place and space; habitat; series

COLLECT
under words
  underpants
  under age
  under cover
  under current
  under fire
  under dressed
  under hand
  under canvas
  under a spell
  underlay
  undercoat
  under the weather
  undertaker
  underdog

VISIT
an underground railway
Sea World or another aquarium and walk under the water
a subway or underpass
a cave
a tunnel
a bridge
a campsite

INVESTIGATE
what is under…?
  our feet
  the bed
  the carpet
  the rotting log
  the rock
  our skin
  the hill
  our hair…

What happens when you bury: wood, metal, plastic, rubbish, or a dead bird?

a microscope
a magnifyer
cross section books – under the ship's deck, under the ramparts
under undergound – the soil
make mud pies,pots, soil castles…
some local undergrowth
what the 'Underground Railway' meant to African Americans
burial customs

animals that live or burrow underneath – gerbils, rabbits, moles, hamsters, bumble bees, worms, ants…
food that is grown underground – carrots, potatoes, onions, radishes, leeks…
transport that travels underneath – tube, submarine, lift, narrow boat…
people who work underneath – coal miner, gold miner, tube driver, deep sea diver…

QUESTIONS WORTH ASKING
How do animals survive underground or underwater?
Why do animals choose to make homes underground?
How far do you have to travel to be underneath?
Does there have to be an over in order to go under?
How far can you go under?

BOOKS

Ships (Look Inside Cross Sections)
Moira Butterfield

Tickly Under There
Debi Gliori

The Armadillo Under My Pillow
Chris White

The Bear Under the Stairs
Helen Cooper

Under the Stars
Lucy Daniels

What's Under the Bed?
Mick Manning and Brita Granström

What's Under the Sea?
Sophy Tahta

U is for **under**

A learning story

As a result of watching television's Time Team, a class of seven to nine year olds had asked about the nature of archaeological finds: 'Why did the ancient people live underground?' – a quite reasonable question given that everything on the television programme seemed to confirm this.

Discussion followed of how things get buried in the first place, where the soil comes from that buries them, how finds are interpreted, what things stay unchanged, and what things rot, or corrode, or perish.

We visited a museum and looked at the oldest objects from Ancient Egypt, recording what most of these objects were made of, and found that stone, metal, glass and ceramics were materials that still exist today almost as fresh as the day they were made, up to 5000 years ago. We concluded that these materials, originating from the planet itself, were durable.

We found few or no objects made of leather, cloth or paper or wood, and although the Ancient Egyptian cases had some materials like papyrus scrolls, and wooden figures and models, stone and glass objects outnumbered them. We concluded that these natural materials were fragile, and noted that the fragile materials had all once been living things.

In the galleries, surrounded by the collection, I explained the Ancient Egyptian belief in an afterlife as a place as lovely as the banks of the Nile, but where every necessity from this life would have to be taken along. I confessed that, if put into that position today, I would have to take my hair dryer, and asked what their own list of necessities would be, clarifying that nothing would be provided, everything would have to be taken. Games, food, pets, and toiletries were all suggested, and to their delight we were able to find equivalent ancient objects in the collection, and reflected that we were not so very different, three to five thousand years later.

I told the emotional story of Isis and Osiris, and of the origins and process of mummification; of the necessity for the removal of the organs and their storage in four canopic jars with lids of the heads of the four sons of Horus and of the weighing of the heart ceremony.

The story of the weighing of the heart ceremony enthralled the children. Papyri illustrated the heart being weighed on a pan on giant scales, against the feather of truth in the other pan. Those who had followed the ways of the gods would have hearts as light as the feather of Ma'at, but those who had followed an evil path would have heavy hearts and never reach the afterlife, as their hearts would be devoured by the part-crocodile, part-hippopotamus, part-lion monster, who was waiting alongside the scale. Some children commented that basically similar ideas about living a good life and going to heaven were held by world religions today.

In the classroom, we sorted and classified everyday objects in the room according to origins – once-living, or from the planet, and made predictions based on the museum collection as to which objects would be durable and still be around in 5000 years time, and which would not even be around in five days/weeks/months/years time. We further sorted objects into natural or manufactured; the manufactured objects were sorted according to raw materials of origin, and this always led back to natural or planetary origin.

Clay as a raw material was investigated, including its geological origins; we dug some from the ground as evidence. Clay objects were made (Egyptian shawabtis, scarabs, and heads of the four sons of Horus – a man, a baboon, a jackal, and a hawk – as lids for canopic jars). These were dried and fired, to demonstrate irreversible change, while some clay was simply dried, and recycled by adding water, to demonstrate reversible change.

A dance was made about the life, death and mummification of the pharaoh, and his passing to the afterlife, by splitting the class into four groups of eight, to include two pharaohs and attendants. Taking inspiration from tomb paintings in the British Museum of hunting scenes along the banks of the Nile, we created a lively set of running and spear-throwing sequences punctuated by still, profile poses. After the pharaoh's death, he was rowed rhythmically across the Nile with great dignity from east to west to the mummy maker's workshop, and mourned by attendants rhythmically scooping and throwing sand over their heads, as depicted in tomb paintings.

The pharaoh was mummified with respect and gravitas by the attendants, taking care to sequence the bandaging of limbs, and rolling the body over, which took cooperation across the entire group.

With the final opening of the mouth ceremony, pharaoh arrived in the afterlife, and with attendants, resumed the hunting sequences that had opened the dance, coming to an end with a final tableau of static profile poses, again selected from wall paintings. The accompanying music was from the CD Ankh: *The Sound of Ancient Egypt*, produced by musicologists recreating ancient Egyptian music from what evidence remains, from which I selected and spliced to create a single piece of appropriate lively and rhythmic passages contrasting with mournful and solemn passages appropriate to the dance sections. Its strange and unfamiliar sounds helped to create an atmosphere of other-worldness, as well as inform and enhance the qualities of the dance.

We observed how quickly natural materials can rot away by watching courgettes and lettuce in sealed see-through bags, as compared to dried pulses, and grains, and deduced that wetness had a lot to answer for in the speed of rotting – hence the mummy makers extracting the viscera from the body and storing them in jars, to preserve the body.

We played a variety of games, learned at an inset session with a museum educator. Some were more difficult to grasp than others, but all intrigued and compelled the children, especially a simplified version of 20 questions which we played every afternoon before going home.

The Question-It game involved children in pairs back to back, one of whom held an everyday object. The other child couldn't see it but tried to figure out what it was by asking questions about it. Most started by stabbing at wild guesses (optimistically – 'Is it a dog?') but quickly learned to refine their questioning technique using elimination by category ('Is it natural or was it made?'), comparison of, for example size ('Is it bigger than a pencil case?'), weight ('Is it heavier than a pencil? Heavier than a dictionary?'), and raw materials ('Was it ever alive, or made of the planet?'), as well as sensory attributes like texture, colour, smell, and any sounds it might afford. Developing fluency with attributes like rigid, flexible, elastic, flimsy, brittle, transparent, opaque, was deeply meaningful in this context, as were geometric terms like symmetrical and asymmetrical, solid, hollow, spherical, cuboid, cylindrical.

Another game involved elaborately upholstered feely-boxes with curtained windows through which to push the hand, with velcro stickers lining the walls that I (or they in partners) attached velcro'd objects to, and could keep changing. They would either draw the objects, and then try to figure out which was which when the objects were displayed, or they would try to describe the object/s to a partner, who would try to draw them. The hilarity and fun of these games didn't detract from the deep learning that was going on, based on the tactile sensory experience and reasoning. The names of the regular solid shapes (cylinder, tetrahedron, cuboid and so forth) were brought to life for children as these terms were essential to describing the objects. Dozens of different prepositions got a very good airing too.

There was nowhere that we could properly excavate on our urban, Victorian-era site, largely given over to tarmac and paving, but we swept a grassy border with a child's metal detector, and experienced the exhilaration of an authentic 'find', not more than an inch below the turf – a ring pull.

So that the children could experience an archaeological dig, and simulate the way that real archaeologists work, I filled large plastic storage boxes, at least two and a half feet deep by two and a half feet wide and long, with moistened sand, and a variety of objects, to be excavated by a group of four children at a time.

I contrived to make three distinct layers of finds for the children in the boxes, representing three distinct eras (ancient, distant past, recent past), separated by layers of moist sand with parts of, or entire objects made of stone, or metal, or glass, or ceramic, in the lowest layer.

The middle layer held objects made of wood, leather, bone, and the layer nearest the surface held plastics, polystyrene, modern ceramics and bits of cloth, wax, and natural objects like cones.

The boxes were divided into quadrants and numbered, and the children were given paper to mark which quadrant their finds came from and also which layer. Compasses attached to the box told them which direction was north, essential for mapping their finds correctly.

A section of the room was given over to the archaeologists' 'laboratory', with washing bowl, rulers, weighing scales, magnifiers, drawing paper and pencils, and clipboards, so they could wash, dry, weigh, measure, and draw their finds from observation.

Excavation was carried out with plastic teaspoons and paintbrushes, and the only two difficulties were training them to scrape the sand horizontally rather than dig all the objects out in one session, and to keep adult hands out of the pits, as adults found the experience as compelling as the children. The sand was excavated into bowls and emptied into the nursery sandpit.

This imaginative activity was arresting on many levels:
• the methodical scraping away of layers like a real archaeologist
• the anticipation of a 'find'
• the hope against hope that they might unearth skeletons
• the exhilaration of the first exposure of an object, and the predictions as to what it might be ('Do you think it's a skeleton?')
• the gleeful extraction of the find from its 'stratum'
• the reverence it was accorded as it was recorded on the pit plan, cleaned, weighed, measured, drawn, and speculations made as to its function.

There was much discussion about the function of unfamiliar objects (roughly one in five objects was unfamiliar) amongst the four children sharing the pit, and based around these questions:
'Do you think it's the whole thing you've found, or a part?'
'Have you ever seen anything like it?'
'If you had one, what would you use it for?'
Finds were analysed in the same way as in the games earlier described, to try to deduce purpose – decorative or functional? Or both? Their finds and conclusions were recorded on bar graphs.

Overall, this exploration occupied the equivalent of two afternoons a week for about half a term, and covered learning in science, DT, art, dance, history, geography, English, RE and maths. But the whole was greater than the sum of its parts, based as it was in experiences that were first hand, experiences that were compelling and cumulative in their impact, and in the dovetailing of developing knowledge, understanding and skills from across the curriculum, normally separated by subject boundaries.

Next time, I would try embalming a supermarket chicken, to experience at first hand how it worked for the Egyptian embalmers, and I would record more of the children's questions and comments as we went along.

V is for variety

V is for variety

WHAT MATTERS TO CHILDREN what the world is made of; knowing the world; tasting the world

CONNECTIONS WITH
A is for apple
B is for ball, bags, brushes
C is for collections
D is for doors
F is for furniture
H is for homes

...living in the orchard and being hungry and plucking the fruit.
Denise Levertov

BELLS
tinkle, ring, clash, chime, peel, clang, whiz, pop, ding

DO
make a patchwork quilt
record the different voices of water
cook different pasta shapes and eat them (or potatoes, rice, lentils, beans)
plan and perform a variety show
mix and eat a salad
find and draw the differences between four pine cones; oak leaves; big toes; spoons

VISITS AND VISITORS
museum
zoo
rock pools
pet shop
aquarium
botanic garden
garden centre
places of worship
seashore
ponds
toy shop
woods
Balinese Gamelan orchestra
symphony orchestra
choir
litter of kittens

BOOKS
Amazing Grace — Mary Hoffman
Flanimals — Ricky Gervais
House for a Hermit Crab — Eric Carle
Pizza — Jan Pienkowski
Tar Beach — Faith Ringgold

MOVEMENTS
creep, linger, crawl, amble, run, sprint, dawdle, slide, slither, step, lurch, dance, tip-toe, spin, jump, leap, spring

QUESTIONS WORTH ASKING
Do fish sing?
Do trees sing?
Can you make blue?
Does everything have a voice?
Is every Monday the same?
Can you have the same again?
Are two of anything exactly the same?

INVESTIGATE
an orchard
clouds
fingerprints
language
voices
lines
coins
blue
papers
sounds
bells
spices
flavours
cooking pots
a place with no variety

BIG IDEAS
diversity
uniqueness

Glory be to God for dappled things.
Gerard Manley Hopkins

VOICES
speaking whistling singing humming shouting grunting squeaking howling whispering growling

There is merit in variety itself. It provides more points of contact with life, and leads away from uniformity and monotony. Liberty Hyde Bailey

INTERESTING WORDS
similar
same
identical
different
distinctive
special
multiple
repetition

V is for variety
A learning story

A newly amalgamated junior, infant and nursery school held an art exhibition to celebrate the opening of a beautiful new building linking the schools together. The new building is called The Link and so the theme of the exhibition was Links.

A variety of starting points and media were used to stimulate the art created by the children.

In the nursery the children made clay tiles impressed with leaves from the trees around the school. The tiles were linked together with string through holes in the corners.

Four and five year olds explored the properties of buttons and used them to inspire designs for prints and photograms.

A visiting artist, Jane Thewlis, worked with the six year old children to make beautiful sculptures using leaves 'sewn' together with pine needles. These were hung against the windows allowing the light to filter through and enabling the viewer to see beyond, thus linking the inside with the outdoors.

The children aged seven years made a collage of photographs taken of places around the school. The collage then became a starting point for further work including observational drawing on sheets of acetate.

In the next two classes the eight year olds made weavings to reflect the colours and textures of the local environment and also pastel drawings of chains. Only the three primary colours were used for these, blending two primaries to make secondary colours at the point of contact between the links.

The nine year olds used screen-printing to show a range of bridge designs – suspension, cantilever, swing, single and multi span arches – linking places separated by water, rail and road.

Nine and ten year olds explored the paper cut-outs of Henri Matisse. Using a computer art programme, they showed how each shape could be placed in relationship to the others to create individual interpretations of the original.

The oldest children in the school, aged eleven, used the centrepiece of the Sistine Chapel, where Michelangelo shows God reaching out to Adam at the moment of creation, to look at hands: the ways in which we express feelings by touching, stroking, clasping, linking, holding, slapping and shaking hands. The drawings were large, expressive and beautiful.

The school became an art gallery and the children showed each other, their parents and other visitors around, sharing and celebrating their achievements.

This story of 'variety' could be connected through the theme of Links to J is for joining, and through the art gallery theme to T is for Tate and other galleries.

W is for windows

> **WHAT MATTERS TO CHILDREN**   how the world works; things the world is made of

VISIT

places with a variety of windows

- places of worship
- castles
- a greenhouse
- an office block
- boats
- a bird hide
- a lighthouse
- a place with no windows
- the millennium wheels in London and Birmingham

CONNECTIONS

D is for doors

F is for furniture

H is for homes

BIG IDEAS
fitness for purpose, transparency, inside and outside

MAKE

books with windows, flaps, pop-up details
small world play homes and vehicles with windows
large scale structures with windows
peep hole shows using a box
peep hole cameras (from a tin with a pin hole)
role play areas with windows for a purpose:
- a hide to observe wild life
- a lighthouse to beam light
- a bank, post office, or drive through MacDonald's with teller window
- a submersible to explore under the sea
use Miroslav Holub's poem, The Door to inspire thoughts for writing about a window
draw or paint a view from a window

COLLECT

different types of windows; draw and photograph them:

sash	casement
French	bay
dormer	fanlight
skylight	porthole
louvred	windscreen
leaded	stained glass
viewfinder	

More window words

pane	shop window
plate-glass	oriel
mullion	glazing bars
astragal	

More windows in works of art

The Pigeons	Picasso
Open Window at Saint Jeannet	Dufy
The Window	Bonnard
The Garden of Love	Sickert
Open Window, Spitalfields	Eyton
Young Girl in a Green Dress	Matisse

HOW NOT TO DO IT
'Now then, where's the first boy?'
  'Please Sir, he's cleaning the back parlour window,' said the temporary head of the philosophical class.
  'So he is to be sure,' rejoined Squeers. 'We go upon the practical mode of teaching, Nickelby; the regular education system. C-l-e-a-n, clean, verb active, to make bright, to scour. W-i-n, win, d-e-r, der, winder, a casement. When the boy knows this out of book, he goes and does it…'
  Dickens, *Nicholas Nickelby*

QUESTIONS WORTH ASKING

Does a window have to have glass?
Does a window have to open and close?
Are there any windows that are not in buildings?
Why do we need windows?
Do all windows let the light in? Out?
What do windows keep out? In?
When is a window a door?
Who makes windows?
Are our eyes windows? Do people have windows?
Are arrow slits in castles windows?
Are all windows transparent?

INVESTIGATE

window frames – shapes, materials
window panes – materials, function – safety glass, bullet proof, tinted…decoration and style – leaded, stained…
window mechanisms - functions
peep holes, kaleidoscopes, optoscopes
peep hole cameras – image distortion
viewfinders including cameras, camcorders
paper engineering techniques to make windows
windows on the world – telescope, magnifiers, microscope…
how to make your classroom window more interesting
transparency

BOOKS

Dear Zoo	Rod Campbell
Magic Windows	Ernest Nister
Noah's Ark	Sophie Windham
The Tale of the Silver Saucer and the Transparent Apple	Arthur Ransom
The Wheels on the Bus	Paul Zelinsky

Begin challenging your own assumptions. Your assumptions are your windows on the world. Scrub them off every once in a while, or the light won't come in.

Alan Alda

W is for **windows**

X marks the spot

WHAT MATTERS TO CHILDREN making a mark on the world; having an authentic purpose; being in authentic places

MAKE

- a map of the route from where you live to the setting, swimming pool, your favourite place, nearest pillar box, auntie's house...
- a plan of a hamster's cage/goldfish tank/the setting
- a plan of a garden
- bury something in the grounds and make a treasure map for its location
- make a treasure island out of mod roc
- make a clay island with volcanoes and caves and rivers
- make an island out of hessian – gathered, puckered, shredded, plaited
- make an island out of papers – scrunched, twisted, torn, folded
- a bird's eye view of a route in pencil, paint and in 3-D in clay and dance

QUESTIONS WORTH ASKING

If the world's a sphere, why are maps flat?

Why is north at the top and south at the bottom?

Could you get to places by only turning right?

How does Superman know which way to go? (Or Batman or Spiderman?)

Children are moved by an unlimited curiosity and by a great and innate desire to know and to discover. Loris Malaguzzi

MARK WITH AN 'X'

where you live and others live   where you've been

where you were born   where your relatives were born

how tall you are on the wall

BIG IDEAS

scale

aerial perspective (or bird's eye view)

projections

representation and mapping

INVESTIGATE

who uses maps

how birds find their way to and from Africa

how sailors find their way across the ocean

how animals find their way from place to place

(what about moles? worms? fish?)

how pilots find their way in the dark or fog

different projections of the world – Peter's projection and Mercator projection

maps and aerial photographs

metal detectors

emergency exit maps, town maps, city maps, county maps, country maps, continent maps, world maps, ocean to moon and star maps

what 'x' means on:
a container; a birthday card; a register; pieces of work marked by a teacher

what else marks the spot – for example, H for helicopters

what does the skull and cross-bones mean?

BOOKS

At the Crossroads	Rachel Isadora
Arf and the Metal Detector	Philip Wooderson
Penelope and the Pirates	James Young
The Lost Treasure of Captain Blood	Jonathan Stroud
Treasure Hunt	Allan Ahlberg
Wild Will	Ingrid Schubert
Zigby Hunts for Treasure	Brian Paterson

COLLECT

keys from different maps and compare symbols

architects' plans of buildings

old maps

plans of gardens

maps of the stars, depths of the sea

VISIT

a cartographer

garden design studio

architect's office/studio

dance studio

archaeological dig

mountain rescuer

X marks the spot

A learning story

My school is in an urban area. I work with six and seven year olds.

On Monday we went on an autumn walk around the school to look for unusual things.

Our search began in the area immediately outside the classroom door. The children found all manner of treasures. They were surprised to find flowers, as it was late in the year. They identified other unusual objects such as interesting stones, leaves and shapes on the playground. Some children speculated that they had actually found a Viking settlement in the wildlife area; others claimed their treasures were fossils and Roman pottery. One child noticed an area of particularly green grass shaped in a crescent and children considered why this might be. They discussed the ideas of a trench causing it, or fairies, or drains on the playground, or even portholes to Australia or another world.

Then one child said, 'Sometimes you can find buried treasure. Sometimes it is marked with a cross.' Immediately the emphasis moved to a treasure hunt. I had secretly buried some treasure in the school grounds, marking the place with two crossed sticks. I covered two giant sized sweet tubes with foil and filled them with gold foil wrapped chocolate money. I added mystery by marking initials on the foil and randomly decided upon 'S' and 'W'. When someone discovered the spot marked 'X', the children were keen to start digging straight away. They considered whether or not to inform the head teacher of their find and get permission to dig. While some thought not, others thought we should, 'In case she had buried it.' One suggested that we all crowd around the treasure to prevent the head teacher from seeing us when we dug. Another suggested simply digging it up and putting it back, like archaeologists have to. Eventually some children went to get digging tools and some went to get permission, but the tools arrived first and digging began. Within seconds the treasure was unearthed and the children gazed at the cylinders and discussed who might have buried the treasure. Ideas included:

'A burglar put it there.'

'It might belong to someone from a country that begins with SW who crept into our school in the dead of night and stole something. Then they buried it and put an X on top of it and will come back later.'

'It could be a bullet from the war.'

'It's a dinosaur fossil.'

'A secret code.'

'It's sweets, because it begins with SW.'

'Father Christmas could have buried it – Santa Winter.'

'It might be a letter to check that children have been good at school.'

'There might be a carrot inside, because of the shape.'

On Tuesday children continued to handle the tube and speculate as to what the treasure might be.

'It's a letter.'

'A crystal – a big one.'

'Gems.'

'Dynamite!'

'Perhaps it is a rainmaker.'

'It could be a drum because it's a hard shake.'

'It's to do with Father Christmas and his coat is inside, to prove he is real and he has sent a present for everyone. He made us find it because he is magic.'

'It might be Barnaby Bear. He could be magic and change shape so that he could fit in.'

'I would like it to be real.'

Some children thought that, when shaken, the sound reminded them of Maltesers, while others thought the tube was too light, and the sound wasn't right.

When the cylinder was opened the chocolate coins were revealed. Should the children eat them? The answer was almost a unanimous 'YES, eat them.' Some wondered if this was really the right thing to do, and whether the treasure belonged to them. Should they have opened it? The deed was done. Children suggested asking all the teachers and children whose names have 'WS' or 'SW' if it was theirs. 'We could take one coin round to each class and ask if it is theirs.' 'We could share the coins out with all the children in school.' 'We could put it in the paper.' They decided to send a letter to each class and make posters about a find, to display around the school. They set a time limit to claiming the treasure. The capsule was deposited in the school safe until Friday.

By Friday no-one had claimed the treasure, and so at the end of the day, the bounty was shared by all.

On Monday one child brought in a map aged with teabags and singed at the edges made at home with his father. And a week of map-making began…

Y is for yesterday

BIG IDEAS

**change and unchangeableness
similarity and difference
time   style**

VISITS AND VISITORS

people with stories to tell about their memories (everyone has stories to tell)

museums – dinosaurs, transport, armour, costume, childhood…

living history museums

old places – houses, churches, castles, ruins, temples, bridges, caves…

burial places

*History says, Don't hope
On this side of the grave.
But then, once in a lifetime,
The longed – for tidal wave
Of justice can rise up
And hope and history rhyme.*
                    Sophocles

MAKE A TIME CAPSULE FOR TODAY

What will you put in it? – DVD; photos of yourself, your family, your home; newspaper; music…?
Where will you keep it?
When will you open it?

MEMORY

What is memory?

Read *Wilfrid Gordon McDonald Partridge* by Mem Fox.

Make a memory box for yourself. What will you put in it to help you remember?

What are souvenirs? Do you have any?

How do you remember:

  your last birthday?

  a day out?

  a holiday?

  your grandad?

Play Kim's Game and Pairs to practise remembering.

YESTERDAY WORDS

today, tomorrow, before, after, soon, now, then, last night, last week, last year, last summer, a long time ago, yesterday, once upon a time, since then, days of yore

FINDING OUT ABOUT YESTERDAY

look at paintings

Haymaking	Pieter Breughel
The Doctor	Sir Luke Fildes
The Boyhood of Raleigh	Sir John Everett Millais

read stories about the past or with pictures set in the past

make a role play area of an archaeological camp and decide what tools you need

what can you find out from broken and incomplete objects?

find a place where you can do a dig

look at old family photos

BOOKS

Do Knights Take Naps?	Kathy Tucker
Little Stowaway	Theresa Tomlinson
Mockingbird	Allan Ahlberg and Paul Howard
My Grandmother's Clock	Geraldine McCaughrean
Roxaboxen	Alice McLerran
The Grandad Tree	Trish Cooke
When Grandma Came	Jill Paton Walsh

LOOK AT THINGS MADE IN THE PAST

What do you know about them?

What do you know for certain?

What do you think might be true?

How will you find out more?

(see also M is for mysterious objects)

look at 'then and now' photos and spot the differences and likenesses

QUESTIONS WORTH ASKING

What is yesterday? When was yesterday's yesterday?
How many yesterdays are there? What does old look like?
What is time? How old is water?

Imagination is remembering with a special kind of intensity.
                    Jill Pirrie

Y is for yesterday

Learning stories

Learning story one

Working in a mixed age class with children from four to six, the Yesterday project fitted nicely into the theme on family history, which was part of the school's rolling plan. It offered many opportunities for numeracy (sequencing events, using vocabulary to describe time) and literacy (re-telling stories, making books, stories with similar settings, recognising question marks and question words). In my weekly planning, which I share with my teaching assistant and pin on the board for parents to look at; I put a list of 'questions worth asking', mostly taken from the sheet. Using the sheet helped me to keep focused on the idea of WHAT MATTERS TO CHILDREN?

Timeline activity

I asked the children to draw a picture of 'something that happened a long time ago', and then we arranged the pictures in order of time. There was a wide variety in their responses: some drew the same picture as always (my birthday, my family, my holiday); many thought quite deeply about 'something that happened a very long time ago'. Some children were confused about when their chosen event happened: were they two, three, four? – while others were very precise: 'My birthday party was at the same time that Fatima was on holiday.' The older children were pleasantly competitive about who could get the first entry: Billy really thought he'd won with 'When Great Aunt Molly was a little girl. Because, she's the oldest person in our family.' He was very crestfallen when Adam came up with, 'Life before man.'

Our yesterday timeline

I asked the children to draw a picture of something that happened a long time ago. I recorded what they said about their picture and they positioned their pictures on a timeline. We left a very large space at the end for 'tomorrow'.

This is when nobody is alive on earth or water, not even an ant or a shark.

Lizards a long time ago before there were people.

When Great-Aunt Molly was a little girl. She's the oldest person in our family.

When my mum was a baby Nanna and Poppa looked after her.

When my mum was little a big boy threw a stone at her. She was a schoolgirl.

My mum and dad got married.

My mum and dad got married in New Zealand.

When I was in my mummy's tummy.

After I popped out of my mum's tummy.

When I was a baby I was in a cot.

I was a baby.

I sat on my sister's lap when I was zero.

I was a baby when Oliver and Charles were little boys.

When I was a baby Billy was only little.

A long time ago my uncle came to see me when I was a baby.

When I was a baby I went to the beach on a rainy day.

It's raining and I'm on the beach holding an ice cream. I was one year old.

When it was Christmas my brother and sister woke me up. I was two.

I went fishing and I didn't catch any fish. I was three.

When it was my fourth birthday.

My old school before I came to this school. It was called Britannia Village. My dad worked there.

I went fishing with my grandpa and my dad a long time ago when I lived in Utah, last summer. I caught a whale with a grown-up hook.

It was my birthday.

I went on holiday last week.

I am going to school today.

...TOMORROW

Learning story two

The story box project

I asked all the children to bring in a story from home, from the childhood of one of their parents (or about themselves when they were small). If they wished they could bring in a box and props to help them tell the story. The parents were very excited about it, and many of them put a lot of work into making a box with their children. Two of the children knew what story they would tell from the first moment I introduced the project: Mario knew he would tell us about fishing in his father's childhood village in Italy, and Harry had a story from his mother's schooldays.

To begin with a group of children told me their stories from memory and I scribed them onto the computer and printed them out in book form for them to illustrate. We read these to the rest of the class. Every time the children retold the stories they used the same words and phrases. When the stories were printed out they found them easy to read. Some of the children have started to make their own books in the class 'office' – usually more complex than the ones I showed them how to make, using masses of paper and sellotape.

Fatima's story

My mummy lived in Uzbekistan. She lived there. I was born in Uzbekistan. My grandma has a big house. It has a round box with toys in it.

Harry's story

When my mum was a little girl she was at her school. A big boy threw a stone at her. She got a big lump on her forehead. You can still feel that lump on her head now.

Mario's story

When I was little I went to Messina with my dad. I went fishing at night. I saw a dolphin on the way to the place where I was going to fish. I saw a helicopter landing on a volcano. I caught lots of fish. I caught three at a time sometimes. When I got home I ate the fish.

Adam's story

My great grandma told me a story. A long time ago she owned a shop. It was a fruit shop. It was called Tom Heydon. When granddad was a little boy he helped in the shop.

Other 'golden moments' of learning about yesterday came in activities that are old favourites. We played a variation of the game 'My grandmother's cat' called 'My teacher's teddy': the children passed round an old teddy bear of mine, adding an adjective each time:

> My teacher's bear is an old, patched, ripped, dusty, one-eyed, broken bear.

The next day Thomas and Phoebe brought their newer teddies in to compare. Bobby said,

> I can tell they're not old because they're not all those words we said about your bear.

Z is for zig-zag

...finding your way through the book

> This is the final letter of our alphabet and so gives us the opportunity to revisit and re-emphasise some of the key characteristics of the approach to children's learning that underpins the book as a whole.

Children as learners

Acting on the world, touching and tasting it, exploring it, asking questions about it, comparing and contrasting, listening and looking, collecting bits of it, discussing and debating it.

The verbs of learning

Nourishing food for active learners

Living animals and plants, natural materials, intriguing and useful artefacts, interesting people of all ages, big ideas, puzzling ideas, contrasts and consequences, identity and differences.

The nouns of learning

Metaphors for learning

Not a ladder...nor a long-jump ...so that learning can be calibrated, quantified or measured, but an exploration, a journey, a narrative.

Learning stories

We are drawn to the metaphors of journey and narrative as ways of understanding children's learning, but we do not believe that journeys must always follow the same route, or that there is only one ending to a story or only one way to tell it.

The structure of this book invites educators to devise routes and create learning stories of their own invention, following their children's threads of interest in the world around them – a world of shifting seasons and sensations, unpredictable happenings and exhilarating surprises.

The suggestions in this book are not to be followed in strict alphabetical order: we hope educators will discover zig-zag routes of their own, as their children make new connections and build new bridges between different aspects of their learning.

The BIG IDEAS section on each page may be a helpful way of identifying an interesting next step to take – but there is no substitute for paying close attention to children's spontaneous talk, play, drawings and other representations, to see which way the grain of their thinking lies. This kind of attention, listening and looking respectfully, is the key to the educator's responsibility to work 'with the grain', in Annabelle Dixon's memorable phrase, rather than teaching 'across the grain'.

Z is for a zig-zag route through the book

So for example,
an educator might start here:

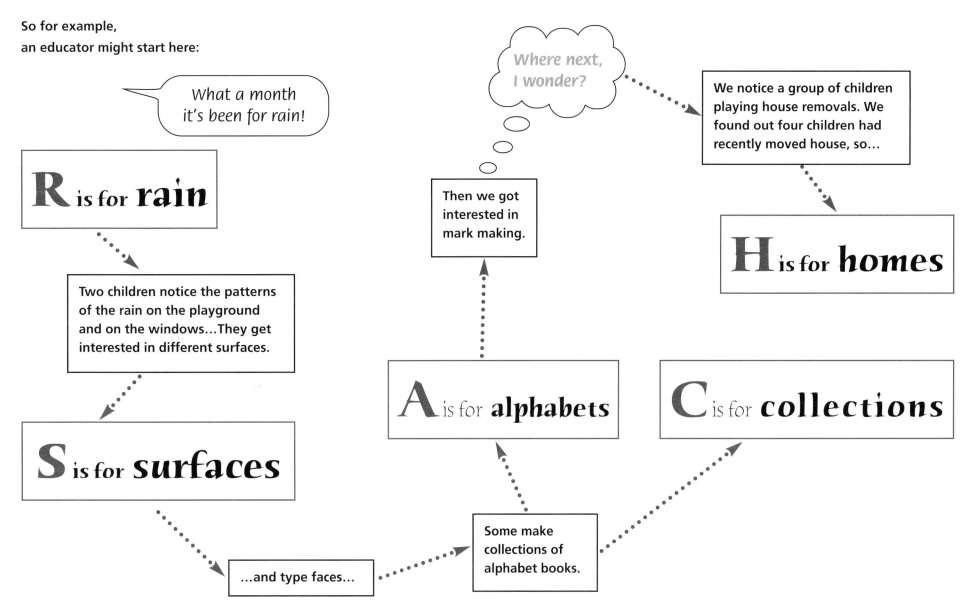

What a month
it's been for rain!

R is for **rain**

Two children notice the patterns
of the rain on the playground
and on the windows...They get
interested in different surfaces.

S is for **surfaces**

...and type faces...

Some make
collections of
alphabet books.

A is for **alphabets**

Then we got
interested in
mark making.

Where next,
I wonder?

We notice a group of children
playing house removals. We
found out four children had
recently moved house, so...

H is for **homes**

C is for **collections**

A is for **afterwards**

...and now it's your turn

?	is for

WHAT MATTERS TO CHILDREN

YOUR CHOICE

INVESTIGATE

YOUR CHOICE

VISIT

YOUR CHOICE

QUESTIONS WORTH ASKING

YOUR CHOICE

BIG IDEAS

References

Books for educators

Adams, S., Alexander, E., Drummond, M.J. and Moyles, J. (2004) *Inside the Foundation Stage: Recreating the Reception Year* London: Association of Teachers and Lecturers

Alda, A. (1980) *62nd Commencement Speech* Connecticut College

Allen of Hurtwood, Lady (1968) *Planning for Play* London: Thames and Hudson

Bailey, L.H. (1922) *The Apple Tree* New York: MacMillan Company

Barnes, R. (1987) *Teaching Art to Young Children 4–9* London: Allen and Unwin

Bissex, G. (1980) *GNYS AT WRK: a child learns to write and read* Cambridge: MA Harvard University Press

Board of Education (1933) *Report of the Consultative Committee on Infant and Nursery Schools* London: HMSO (The Hadow Report)

Boyle Family (1986) *Beyond Image* (Catalogue for the Boyle Family Exhibit) London: Arts Council of Great Britain

Brown, B. (2001) *Combating Discrimination: Persona Dolls in Action* Stoke on Trent: Trentham Books

Carr, M. (2001) *Assessment in Early Childhood Settings: Learning Stories* London: Paul Chapman

Central Advisory Council for Education (1967) *Children and their Primary Schools* London: HMSO (The Plowden Report)

Clarke, A. and Moss, P. (2001) *Listening to Young Children: the Mosaic Approach* London: The Joseph Rowntree Foundation (National Children's Bureau)

Claxton, G. (Spring 2001) *Speech at the Conference for South Hertfordshire Schools*

Cousins, J. (2003) *Listening to Four Year Olds* London: National Early Years Network

Department for Education and Skills (2003) *Excellence and Enjoyment: a strategy for primary schools* Nottingham: DfES

Department for Training and Education (2003) *The Learning Country: Foundation Phase 3–7 Years* Cardiff: National Assembly for Wales

Department for Education and Employment (2000) *Curriculum Guidance for the Foundation Stage Guidance* London: QCA

Department of Education and Science (1990) *Starting with Quality: The Report of Inquiry into the Quality of the Educational Experiences Offered to 3 and 4 Year Olds* London: HMSO (The Rumbold Report)

Dickens, C. (1995) *Nicholas Nickelby* Ware: Wordsworth Editions Ltd.

Dickens, M and Denziloe J. (2003) *All Together: how to create inclusive services for disabled children and their families* London: National Children's Bureau (second edition)

Drummond, M.J. (1996) *Play, Learning and the National Curriculum: some possibilities in The National Curriculum in the Early Years* London: Falmer Press

Drummond, M.J. (1998) 'Observing Children' in Smidt, S. (ed) *The Early Years: a reader* London: Routledge

Drummond, M. J. (2003) *Assessing Children's Learning* London: David Fulton (second edition)

Durbin, G., Morris, S. and Wilkinson, S. (1990) *Learning from Objects* London: English Heritage

Early Childhood Forum (2003) *Quality in Diversity* London: National Children's Bureau (second edition)

Edwards, C., Gandini, L. and Forman, G. (1993) *The Hundred Languages of Children* Norwood, NJ: Ablex

Edwards, C., Gandini, L. and Forman, G. eds. (1998) *The Hundred Languages of Children: advanced reflections* Greenwich: Ablex (second edition)

Einstein, A. (1959) in *Albert Einstein, Philosopher, Scientist*, Schlipp, P. A . (ed) New York: Harper Torchbooks

Einstein, A. (1973) in Bernstein, J. R. *Einstein* London: Collins

Feynman, R. (1968) 'What is Science?' in *The Physics Teacher* 7.6. 313-20

Fraser, G. and Gestwicki, C. (2002) *Authentic Childhood: Exploring Reggio Emilia in the Classroom* Albany, NY: Delmar Thomson Learning

Gardner, H. (1999) *Intelligence Reframed: Multiple Intelligence for the 21st Century* New York: Basic Books

Graham, M. in National Advisory Council on Creative and Cultural Education (1999) *All Our Futures: Creativity, Culture and Education* London: DES (The Robinson Report)

Griffiths, R. (1930) *A Study of Imagination in Early Childhood* London: Routledge and Kegan Paul

Hodgkin, R. (1985) *Playing and Exploring* London: Methuen

Holt, J. (1990) *How Children Fail* (revised edition) London: Penguin

Holmes, E. in Holmes, G. (1952) *The Idiot Teacher* London: Faber and Faber (reissued by Spokesman, 1977)

Huxley, A. (1962) *Island* London: Chatto and Windus (reissued by Flamingo, 1994)

Isaacs, S. (1929) *The Nursery Years* London: Routledge

Isaacs, S. (1930) *Intellectual Growth in Young Children* London: Routledge and Kegan Paul

Isaacs, S. (1932) *The Children We Teach* London: University of London Press

Jenkinson, S. (2001) *The Genius of Play* Stroud: Hawthorn Press

Lane, J. (2005) *Action for Racial Equality in the Early Years: Understanding the Past, Thinking About the Present, Planning for the Future* London: National Children's Bureau

Learning and Teaching Scotland (2000) *The Structure and Balance of the Curriculum: 5–14 National Guidelines* Dundee: Learning and Teaching Scotland

Learning Through Landscapes (2004) *Vision and Values Statement* www.ltl.org.uk

Levertov, D. (2003) *New Selected Poems* Northumberland: Bloodaxe Books

MacDonald, G. (1982) *Castle Warlock* London: Samson Low

Matisse, H. in Reid, L.A. (1969) *Meaning in the Arts* London: Allen and Unwin

Matthews, G. (1984) *Dialogues with Children* Cambridge, MA: Harvard University Press

Newton, I. in Brewster, D. (1855) *Memories of the Life, Writings and Discoveries of Sir Isaac Newton* Edinburgh: Thomas Constable

Owens, J. and Neimark, P.G. (1978) *Jesse: A Spiritual Autobiography* Plainfield, NJ: Logos International

Nutbrown, C. (1999) *Threads of Thinking: Young Children Learning and the Role of Early Education* London: Paul Chapman (second edition)

Paley, V. G. (1981) *Wally's Stories* Cambridge, MA: Harvard University Press

Paley, V. G. (1984) *Boys and Girls: Superheroes in the Doll Corner* Chicago: University of Chicago Press

Paley, V. G. (1999) *The Kindness of Children* Cambridge, MA: Harvard University Press

Paley, V. G. (2004) *A Child's Work: The Importance of Fantasy Play* London: Heinemann

Piaget, J. (1951) *Play, Dreams and Imitation in Childhood* London: Heinemann

Piaget, J. (2002) *The Language and Thought of the Child* London: Routledge Classic (first published in Paris, 1923)

Pirrie, J. (1987) *On Common Ground: a Programme for Teaching Poetry* London: Hodder and Stoughton

Qualifications and Curriculum Authority (2000) *Curriculum Guidance for the Foundation Stage* London: QCA/DfES

Reggio Children (1996) *The Hundred Languages of Children* (exhibition catalogue) Reggio Emilia: Reggio Children

Rinaldi, C. (1998) 'Projected Curriculum Constructed Through Documentation-Progettazione' in Edwards, C., Gandini, L. and Forman, G. (eds) *The Hundred Languages of Children: The Reggio Emilia Approach – advanced reflections* Greenwich, CT.: Ablex (second edition)

Roberts, R. (ed) (2000) *Learning Together With Fours* Oxford: PEEP

Schiller, C. (1979) in Griffin Beale, C. (ed) *Christian Schiller in his Own Words* London: A. and C. Black

Schools Council (1981) *Resources for Visual Education 7–13* London: Schools Council Art Committee

Scottish Consultative Council on the Curriculum (1999) *A Curriculum Framework for Children 3–5* Dundee: Scottish Consultative Council on the Curriculum

Sophocles 'The Cure at Troy', in *Philoctetes* (1990) translated by Seamus Heaney, London: Faber and Faber

von Oech, R. (1992) *A Whack on the Side of the Head: How You Can be More Creative* Boston, MA: Walker Books

Wells, G. (1987) *The Meaning Makers: Children Learning Language and Using Language to Learn* London: Heinemann

Books for children

Adelman, B. (1999) *Roy Lichtenstein's ABC* London: Bulfinch Press

Ahlberg, A. (2002) *Treasure Hunt* London: Walker Books Ltd.

Ahlberg, A. and Howard, P. (1999) *Mockingbird* London: Walker Books Ltd.

Ahlberg, A. and J. (1999) *Cops and Robbers* London: Penguin

Ahlberg, A. and J. (2003) *Peepo!* London: Viking Books

Allen, J. (1993) *Who's at the Door?* New York: Tambourine

Andersen, H. C. (1999) *The Ugly Duckling* London: Orchard Books

Andreae, G. (2000) *Giraffes Can't Dance* London: Orchard Books

Anholt, L. (1996) *Magpie Song* London: Egmont Books

Anholt, L. (2003) *Camille and the Sunflowers* London: Frances Lincoln Ltd.

Anholt, L. (2003) *Degas and the Little Dancer* London: Frances Lincoln Ltd.

Anholt, L. (2003) *Picasso and the Girl with a Ponytail* London: Frances Lincoln Ltd.

Anno, M. (1974) *Anno's Alphabet* London: Bodley Head

Anno, M. and Anno, M. (1983) *Anno's Mysterious Multiplying Jar* New York: Philomel Books

Armitage, D. and R. (1994) *The Lighthouse Keeper's Lunch* London: Scholastic Hippo

Baker, J. (1989) *Where the Forest Meets the Sea* London: Walker Books Ltd.

Baker, J. (2002) *Window* London: Walker Books Ltd.

Barber, A. (1990) *The Mousehole Cat* London: Walker Books Ltd.

Barrie, J.M. (2004) *Peter Pan and Wendy* Dorking: Templar (centenary edition)

Base, G. (2004) *The Water Hole* London: Puffin

Bender, R. (1994) *A Most Unusual Lunch* New York: Dial Books

Bjork, C. (1987) *Linnea in Monet's Garden* Stockholm: R and S Books

Blake, Q. (2000) *The Green Ship* London: Red Fox

Blizzard, G.S. (1992) *Animals in Art (Come Look with Me)* Charlottesville, VA: Thomasson-Grant

Blizzard, G.S. (1996) *Exploring Landscape Art with Children (Come Look with Me)* Charlottesville, VA: Thomasson-Grant

Bolliger, M. (1976) *The Giant's Feast* Reading, MA: Addison-Wesley

Bradman, T. (1990) *The Sandal* London: Puffin

Breeze, L. (1998) *Pickle and the Ball* New York: Larousse Kingfisher Chambers

Brett, J. (1993) *The Mitten* London: Hodder Wayland

Briggs, R. (1978) *The Snowman* London: Hamish Hamilton

Brighton, C. (2000) *Fossil Girl* London: Frances Lincoln Ltd.

Brown, M. W. (2002) *Sailor Boy Jig* New York: Margaret K. McElderry Books

Brown, R. (1992) *A Four-Tongued Alphabet* London: Random House Children's Books

Brown, R. (1997) *If At First You Do Not See* London: Andersen Press

Brown, R. (2000) *Snail Trail* London: Andersen Press

Browne, A. (1990) *Change* London: Julia MacRae Books

Browne, E. (1995) *Handa's Surprise* London: Walker Books Ltd.

Burningham, J. (1988) *Grandpa* London: Puffin

Burningham, J. (2004) *The Magic Bed* London: Random House Children's Books

Butterfield, M. (1994) *Ships (Look Inside Cross Sections)* London: Dorling Kindersley

Campbell, R. (1999) *Dear Zoo* New York: Simon and Schuster

Carle, E. (1991) *A House for a Hermit Crab* New York: Aladdin Picture Books

Carle, E. (1997) *The Tiny Seed* London: Puffin

Carle, E. (1998) *Little Cloud* London: Puffin

Carle, E. (1998) *The Mixed up Chameleon* London: Puffin

Carle, E. (1999) *Roosters Off to See the World* New York: Aladdin Picture Books

Carle, E. (2002) T*he Very Hungry Caterpillar* London: Puffin

Cartwright, R. (1995) *James and the Rain* New York: Simon and Schuster

Chichester Clark, E. (2001) *Follow My Leader* London: Harper Collins

Churchill, V. (2003) *Sometimes I Like to Curl Up in a Ball* London: Gullane Children's Books

Clement, R. (1999) *Frank in Time* Sydney: Angus and Robertson Children's Books

Cole, B. (2001) *Drop Dead* London: Red Fox

Cooke, T. (2000) *The Grandad Tree* London: Walker Books Ltd.

Cooper, H. (1999) *Pumpkin Soup* London: Random House Children's Books

Cooper, H. (2002) *The Bear Under the Stairs* London: Red Fox

Cooper, S. (2003) *Frog* London: Random House Children's Books

Cox, P. (2001) *An Abstract Alphabet* San Francisco: Chronicle Books

Curtis, J. L. (1999) *Tell Me Again About the Night I was Born* London: Scholastic Children's Books

Daniels, L. (2000) *Under the Stars* London: Hodder and Stoughton

Donaldson, J. (2002) *Room on the Broom* London: Macmillan Children's Books

Drummond, A. (1992) *The Willow Pattern Story* New York:
   North South Books

Fearnley, J. (2003) *Billy Tibbles Moves Out!* London: Harper Collins

Foreman, M. (1993) *Dinosaurs and All That Rubbish* London: Penguin

Forward, T. (2000) *Once Upon an Everyday* London: Doubleday

Fox, M. (1984) *Wilfrid Gordon McDonald Partridge* New York:
   Kane / Miller

French, V. (2001) *Growing Frogs* London: Walker Books Ltd.

Geraghty, P. (1996) *The Hunter* London: Random House Children's
   Books

Geraghty, P. (2003) *Over the Steamy Swamp* London: Red Fox

Gervais, R. (2004) *Flanimals* London: Faber and Faber

Gliori, D. (2002) *Tickly Under There* London: Orchard

Guinness Book of Records 2005 50th anniversary edition (2004)
   New York: Time Inc Home Entertainment

Hanson, P. (2003) *My Granny's Purse* New York: Workman Publishing

Haswell, P. (1994) *It's Now or Never* London: Red Fox

Haughton, E. (2000) *Rainy Day* London: Transworld Publishers

Henderson, K. (1992) *In the Middle of the Night* London:
   Walker Books Ltd.

Henderson, K. (1997) *The Little Boat* London: Walker Books Ltd.

Henderson, K. (2000) *The Storm* London: Walker Books Ltd.

Hoban, R. (1986) *The Rain Door* London: Gollancz

Hoffman, M. (1991) *Amazing Grace* New York: Dial Books

Hoffman, M. (2001) *The Colour of Home* London: Frances Lincoln Ltd.

Hughes, S. (1979) *Dogger* London: Picture Lions

Hughes, S. (2004) *Alfie's Feet* London: Red Fox

Hutchins, P. (2002) *Don't Forget the Bacon* London:
   Random House Children's Books

Inkpen, M. (1996) *Nothing* London: Hodder Children's Books

Isadora, R. (1993) *At the Crossroads* London: Red Fox

Jay, A. (2000) *Alphabet* London: Templar

Jay, A. (2000) *Picture This* London: Templar

Jensen, V. A. (1977) *Sara and the Door* Reading, MA: Addison-Wesley

Jirankova-Limbrick, M. (2003) *The Artful Alphabet* London:
   Walker Books Ltd.

Katzen, M. and Henderson, A. (2004) *Pretend Soup and Other Real
   Recipes* Berkley, CA: Tricycle Press

Kennedy, J. (1995) *Teddy Bears Picnic* London: Blackie

Kerr, J. (2003) *Goodbye Mog* London: Trafalgar Square Books

Kingsley, C. (2003) *The Water Babies* London: Award Publications

Koralek, J. (1994) *The Boy and the Cloth of Dreams* Cambridge, MA:
   Candlewick Press

Lambert, S and S.A. (1997) *Best of Friends* London: Frances Lincoln Ltd.

Lewis, C. S. (1998) *The Lion, the Witch and the Wardrobe* London:
   Harper Collins

Lexa Schaefer, C. (2001) *The Copper Tin Cup* London: Walker Books Ltd.

Lindbergh, R. (1993) *Johnny Appleseed* Boston, MA:
   Megan Tingley Books

Lobel, A. (1994) *The Great Blueness* New York: Harper Collins

Lobel, A. (2004) *Frog and Toad Make a List* in The Frog and Toad
   Collection. New York: Harper Trophy

Locker, T. (2003) *Cloud Dance* New York: Harcourt Children's Books

Lum, K. and Johnson, A. (1998) *What!* London: Bloomsbury

Manning, M and Granstrom, B. (2004) *What's Under the Bed?*
   London: Franklin Watts

Mayhew, J. (2004) *Katie's Picture Show* London: Orchard Books

McAfee, A. (1998) *Why do the Stars Come Out at Night?*
   London: Random House Children's Books

McCaughrean, G. (2003) *My Grandmother's Clock* London:
   Harper Collins

McLerran, A. (2004) *Roxaboxen* London: Harper Trophy

Messenger, N. (2001) *The Creation Story* London: Dorling Kindersley

Micklethwait. L. (1994) *I Spy Animals in Art* London: Picture Lions

Micklethwait. L. (1996) *I Spy Transport in Art* London: Picture Lions

Mitton, T. (2002) *Down by the Cool of the Pool* London:
   Watts Publishing Group

Mitton, T. (2003) *Bumpus Jumpus Dinosaurumpus* London:
   Watts Publishing Group

Moore, I. (2004) *Six Dinner Sid* London: Hodder Children's Books

Munro, R. (2004) *Doors* Zurich: North-South Books

Munsch, R. N. (2003) *The Paper Bag Princess* London: Scholastic Press

Nascimbeni, B. (2000) *Big Band* London: Campbell Books

Nesbit, E. (2004) *Five Children and It* UK retold by UK Film Council,
   London: Harper Collins

Nickl, P. (1990) *Crocodile Crocodile* Zurich: North-South Books

Nicholl, H, and Pienkowski, J. (2004) *Meg and Mog* London:Puffin

Nister, E. (1981) *Magic Windows* London: Collins

Obi, A. (2002) *Yohance and the Dinosaurs* London: Tamarind Ltd.

Onyefulu, I. (1996) *A is for Africa* London: Frances Lincoln Ltd.

Onyefulu. I. (2000) *Chidi Only Likes Blue: an African Book of Colours*
    London: Frances Lincoln Ltd.

Orr, R. (1995) *Nature Cross Sections* London: Dorling Kindersley

Paterson, B. (2003) *Zigby Hunts for Treasure* New York: Harper Collins

Paton Walsh, J. (1993) *When Grandma Came* London: Puffin

Patten, B. (1999) *The Blue and Green Planet* London: Scholastic Press

Petricelli, L. (2004) *Big, Little* London: Walker Books Ltd.

Petricelli, L. (2004) *Quiet, Loud* London: Walker Books Ltd.

Petty, K. and Maizels, J. (1999) *The Magnificent I Can Read Music Book*
    London: Random House Children's Books

Petty, K. and Maizels, J. (2000) *The Wonderful World Book* London:
    Random House

Petty, K. and Maizels, J. (2005) *The Global Garden* London:
    Eden Books, Transworld

Philpot, G. and L. (1994) *Amazing Anthony Ant* London:
    Random House Children's Books

Pienkowski, J. (2001) *Pizza* London: Walker Books Ltd.

Pike, N. (1983) *The Peach Tree* New York: Stemmer House Publishers

Pittau, F.and Gervais, B. (2004) *Elephant Elements* London:
    Chrysalis Books

Puttock, S. (2001) *A Ladder to the Stars* London: Frances Lincoln Ltd.

Ransom, A. (1986) 'The Tale of the Silver Saucer and the Transparent
    Apple' in *Old Peter's Russian Tales* London: Puffin

Ray, J, (1997) *Hansel and Gretel* London: Walker Books Ltd.

Riddle, T. (1992) *Careful With That Ball, Eugene!* Oxford:
    Oxford University Press

Ringgold, F. (1996) *Tar Beach* New York: Dragonfly Books

Robertson. M. P. (1999) *Seven Ways to Catch the Moon* London:
    Frances Lincoln Ltd.

Rose, G. (2001) *Hair* London: Anderson Press

Rosen, M. (2000) *We're Going on a Bear Hunt* London:
    Walker Books Ltd.

Ross, T. and Willis, J. (2003) *I Want to be a Cowgirl* London:
    Andersen Press

Say, A. (1991) *Tree of Cranes* Boston, MA: Houghton Mifflin. K.

Schnitzlein, D. (2001) *The Monster Who Ate My Peas* Atlanta, GA:
    Peachtree Publishers

Schubert, I. (1994) *Wild Will* Minneapolis, MN: Carolrhoda Books

Schubert, L. (2000) *Winnie Plays Ball* London: Walker Books Ltd.

Sendak, M. (1986) *The Sign on Rosie's Door* London: Puffin

Sendak, M (1996) *In the Night Kitchen* New York: Harper Collins

Sendak, M. (2000) *Where the Wild Things Are* London: Red Fox

Sharratt, N. (1998) *Ketchup on Your Cornflakes* London: Scholastic

Stickland, H and P. (2004) *Dinosaurs Roar!* Sherbourne: Ragged Bear
    Publishing Ltd.

Stickland, P. (1996) *Dinosaur Stomp! A Monster Pop-up Book* New York:
    Dutton Children's Books

Stojic, M. (2000) *Rain* London: David Bennett Books Ltd.

Stroud, J. (1997) *The Lost Treasure of Captain Blood* London:
    Walker Books Ltd.

Tahta, S. (1994) *What's Under the Sea?* London: Usborne Publishing Ltd.

Tan, S. (2004) *The Lost Thing* S. Melbourne, Victoria:
    Thomas C. Lothian Fry Ltd.

Thomas, F. and Collins, R. (1998) *Supposing* London:
    Bloomsbury Paperbacks

Tolstoy, A. (1989) *The Great Big, Enormous Turnip* London: Mammoth

Tomlinson, T. (1997) *Little Stowaway* London: Jonathan Cape

Traditional *Cinderella*

Traditional *Snow White*

Traditional *The Princess and the Pea*

Traditional *The Three Bears*

Traditional *The Three Little Pigs*

Tucker, K. (2001) *Do Knights Take Naps?* London: Cat's Whiskers

Vernon Lord, J. (1988) *The Giant Jam Sandwich* London: Macmillan

Waddell, M. (1996) *The Big Big Sea* London: Walker Books Ltd.

White, C. (2002) *The Armadillo Under My Pillow* Rotherham:
    The King's England Press

Wilde, O. (1995) *The Selfish Giant* New York: G. P. Putnam's Sons

Willis, J. (2001) *Susan Laughs* London: Random House Children's Books

Windham, S. (1999) *Noah's Ark* London: Macmillan Children's Books

Wolfe, G. (2003) *Oxford First Book of Art* Oxford:
    Oxford University Press

Wooderson, P. (2001) *Arf and the Metal Detector* London:
    A and C Black Ltd.

Young, J. (1990) *A Million Chameleons* Boston, MA:
  Little, Brown and Company
Young, J. (1990) *Penelope and the Pirates* New York: Arcade Publishing
Zelinsky, P. (2002) *The Wheels on the Bus* London: Orchard Books

Poems

Benjamin, F. (1998) *Skip Across the Ocean* London: Frances Lincoln Ltd.
Causley, C. (1990) *Colonel Fazackerley* in Causley, C. Figgie Hobbin.
  London: MacMillan Children's Books (new edition)
de la Mare, W. (1962) *The Listeners* in de la Mare Poems by
  Walter de la Mare. London: Puffin
Foster, J. and Paul, K. (2004) *Monster Poems* Oxford:
  Oxford University Press
Harrison, M. (1988) *The Blue Room* in Edwards, R. Splinters. Oxford:
  Oxford University Press
Holub, M. (1967) *The Door* in Milner, I. and Theiner, G. Selected Poems.
  London: Penguin
Jacobs, J. (1862) *Nix, Nought, Nothing* in English Fairy Tales. London:
  David Nutt (second edition revised)
Hood, T. (1969) *No!* in Kirkup, J. Shepherding Winds. London:
  Blackie and Son Ltd.
Hopkins, G. M (1969) *Pied Beauty* in Mackay, D. A Flock of Words.
  London: Bodley Head
Morgan, E. (1981) *The Apple's Song* in McGough, R. Strictly Private.
  London: Viking Kestrel
McKellar, S. (1997) *A Child's Book of Lullabies* London:
  Dorling Kindersley
Mitton, T. (2002) *Pip* London: Scholastic Press
Mitton, T. (2003) *Green Man Lane* in Mitton, T. Plum: Poems. New York:
  Arthur A. Devine
Monro, H. (2003) *Overheard on a Saltmarsh* in Duffy, C.A.
  Overheard on a Saltmarsh: Poet's Favourite Poems. London:
  Young Picador
Traditional (1989) *The Key to the Kingdom* in Craft, R.
  The Song That Sings the Bird: Poems for Young Children.
  London: Collins Sons and Co Ltd.

Works of art

Balla, G. (1912) *Dynamism of a Dog on a Leash*, oil on canvas.
  Buffalo: Albright Knox Gallery
Balla, G. (1912) *Girl Running on a Balcony*, oil on canvas. Milan:
  Gallery of Modern Art
Boccioni, U. (1913) *Dynamism of a Soccer Player*, oil on canvas.
  New York: Museum of Modern Art
Boccioni, U. (1913) *Unique Forms of Continuity in Space*, bronze.
  New York: Museum of Modern Art
Bonnard, P. (1921) *The Open Window*, oil on canvas. Washington D.C:
  Phillips Collection
Breughel, P. (1565) *Haymaking*, oil on panel. Prague: National Gallery
di Lodovico Buonarroti Simoni, M. (1551) *Creation of Adam*, fresco.
  Rome: Sistine Chapel
Dufy, R. (1928) *The Open Window*, oil on canvas. Chicago: The Art Institute
Eyton, A. (1976-81) *Open Window* Spitalfields, oil on canvas.
  London: Tate Gallery
Fildes L. (Sir) (1891) *The Doctor*, oil on canvas. London: Tate Britain
Gormley, A. (1998) *RhIZome 1*, cast iron. Umea: Sweden
Gormley, A. (1998) *RhIZome 11*, cast iron. Lisbon: Parque Expo
Gormley, A. (2001) *Standing Matter 1, 11, and 111*, forged ball bearing.
  www.anthonygormley.com
Harnett, W. (1988) *My Gems*, oil on wood. Washington D.C.:
  National Gallery of Art
Peto, J. (1865) *Letter Rack*, oil on canvas. New York:
  Metropolitan Museum of Art
Matisse, H. (1921) *Young Girl in a Green Dress*, oil on canvas.
  Private Collection
Millais, J. E. (1870) *The Boyhood of Raleigh*, oil on canvas. London:
  Tate Britain
Picasso, P. (1957) *The Pigeons*, oil on canvas. New York:
  Metropolitan Museum of Art
Pippin, H. (1946) *Victorian Interior*, oil on canvas. New York:
  Metropolitan Museum of Art
Ringgold, F. (1990) *Tar Beach ll*, quilt. Virginia: Museum of Fine Arts
Sickert, W. (1860-1942) *The Garden of Love*, oil on canvas.
  Cambridge: Fitzwilliam Museum
Toyoharu, U. (1739-1816) *Interior and Landscape*, woodblock print.
  Washington D.C.: Freer Gallery

Turner, J.M.W. (1844) *Rain, Steam and Speed*, oil on canvas.
    London: National Gallery
Van Gogh, V. (1889) *The Bedroom at Arles*, oil on canvas. Paris:
    Musee d'Orsay
Van Gogh, V. (1889) *The Starry Night*, oil on canvas. New York:
    Museum of Modern Art

Music

Ankh: The Sound of Ancient Egypt (1998) Michael Atherton,
    Tuscon, AZ: Celestial Harmonies 13174
Heroes and Villains (2004) Brian Wilson, Warner Music Group
I Can't Stand the Rain (1985) Ann Peebles, Capital Records
Nowhere Man (1965) Lennon and McCartney, EMI Records
Purple People Eater (1958) Sheb Wooley, MGM Records
Raindrops Keep Falling on my Head (1970) Bert Bacharach and
    Hal David, Warner Bros.
Prelude no. 15 in D♭ – *The Raindrop* (1810-1849) Chopin
Raining in my Heart (1959) B. and F. Bryant, MCA Records
Romeo and Juliet, Ballet in Four Acts, Op 64 (1934) Prokoviev
4'33" (1993) John Cage John Harrison, Lou Cage, et al.
    Hungaroton Label
Singing in the Rain (1952) Arthur Freed and Nacio Herb Brown CD
    (1996) Rhino Records
Sound of Silence (1965) Paul Simon, CBS Records
Star Wars : A New Hope, Original Motion Picture Soundtrack (1997)
    John Williams, RCA
The Little Fir Tree (2003) James and Joy Wright, Gotalifer Production
The Monster Mash (1962) Bobby Boris Pickett, Universal Music
The Sorcerer's Apprentice (1897) Alexander Dukas
The 1812 Overture in E♭ major, Op 49 (1880) Tchaikovsky
Why Does it Always Rain on me? (1999) Fran Healey, Sony Music

Video and DVD

L'Enfant et les Sortileges (2002) Nederlands Dans Theater Arthaus, on
    Peter and the Wolf Sir Anthony Dowell, The Royal Ballet School and
    L'Enfant et les Sortileges, Nederlands Dans Theater Arthaus DVD
    [2716-DV]
Singing in the Rain (2003) Production Warner Home Video DVD
    [3942-DV]